The Glove Compartment Book

by Joel D. Joseph, J.D.
David Schechter
and
David Greifinger, M.D., M.P.H.

Copyright the National Press, Inc. 1984
5225 Wisconsin Avenue, N.W.
Suite 601
Washington, D.C. 20015

Cover by Sharp & Company

Library of Congress Cataloging in Publication Data

Joseph, Joel D.
  The glove compartment book.

  Includes index.
  1. Automobile driving—Handbooks, manuals, etc.
2. Automobiles—Maintenance and repair—Handbooks,
manuals, etc. 3. Traffic regulations—Handbooks,
manuals, etc. 4. First aid in illness and injury—Handbooks, manuals, etc. I. Greifinger, David, 1947–   .
II. Schechter, David, 1948–   . III. Title.
TL152.5.J67   1984   629.28   84–16651
ISBN 0-915765-04-7 (pbk.)

Contents

Page

1. Introduction   1

Part One—Driver's Legal Manual
2. Insurance   4
3. U.S. Road Signs   9
4. International Road Signs 17
5. Rules of the Road for
   the United States 28
6. Driving in Canada 57
7. International Rules of
   the Road 59
8. What You Should do in Case of an
   Accident in the United States . . . 70
9. What You Should do in Case of an
   Accident Outside the
   United States 83
10. What You Should do When Stopped
    by the Police 85
11. Automobile Warranties 88
12. Buying or Selling a Car 97
13. Automobile Associations
    Throughout the World 103

**Part Two—Driver's Mechanical
Manual**
14. What You Should Always Keep in
    Your Car 110

15. Warning Signs: When You Should not Drive your Car Further........120
16. What you Should Check Before Taking a Trip.............125
17. How to Handle Mechanical Emergencies.............131
18. Changing a Flat Tire..........133
19. Things to do When Car Won't Start 135
20. How to Jump-Start Your Car Safely.................138
21. Towing your Car............140
22. Opening a Frozen Car Door.....141
23. What to do When Your Car Overheats................142
24. What to do When Your Lights Don't Work.................144

Part III—Driver's First Aid Manual

25. Your First-Aid Kit...........148
26. Priority of Treatment........149
27. Back & Neck Injuries........150
28. Bleeding..................153
29. Broken Bones (Fractures)......157
30. Carbon Monoxide Poisoning....161
31. Cardiovascular Resuscitation (CPR) 162
32. Carsickness 164
33. Chest Injuries.............165
34. Diabetes..................167

35. Drowsiness—Warning Signs to
    Stop Driving 168
36. Eye Injuries 170
37. Head Injuries 172
38. Heart Attack 173
39. Nausea & Vomiting 174
40. Pregnancy 175
41. Seizures 177
42. Snowbound Survival 178

Appendix

Emergency Driving 180

Important Information

Name:_____

Address:_____

City:_____State:_____

Driver's License No._____State:_____

Persons to notify in case of accident:

Name:_____

Address:_____

City:_____State:_____

Home Phone:_____Work Phone:_____

Name:_____

Address:_____

City:_____State:_____

Home Phone:_____Work Phone:_____

Insurance Company:_____

Policy Number:_____

Agent's Name:_____

Agent's Telephone No.:_____

Limits of Coverage:_____

Dedication

This book is dedicated to the reduction of traffic-related deaths and injuries.

Acknowledgment

The authors would like to thank the following individual and organizations for their assistance in preparing this book: Edward F. Kearney, the American Automobile Association, the Center for Auto Safety, the National Highway Traffic Safety Administration, the United Nations Educational, Scientific, and Cultural Organization (UNESCO), the Highways Users Federation, the Insurance Institute for Highway Safety, the Traffic Institute, the National Committee on Uniform Traffic Laws and Ordinances and the Washington chanceries of many foreign nations.

Chapter One: Introduction

Before you put this book in your car's glove compartment, look through the book to see the valuable information contained in it. Four chapters that you should read immediately are chapters 14, 15, 25 and 34. These chapters explain the things that you should bring with you in a first aid kit and a mechanical aid kit. Chapter 15 explains warning signs which tell you when not to drive your car any further, to avoid permanent damage to your car or to yourself. And chapter 34 explains when you should stop driving because of drowsiness, or other physical condition.

Read over chapters 17 to 24 regarding mechanical emergencies so that you are generally familiar with it in case you need it for a roadside emergency. From time to time you should look at the pink pages of this book regarding medical emergencies. Because you will not have the time to read every word during an emergency you should know what to expect. The more prepared you are for emergencies the better you will be able to handle them.

Other chapters should be referred to before going on a trip. There is a chapter (chapter six) on driving in Canada. There is a chapter on what you should check before going on a trip (chapter 16). And there is extensive information on driving overseas, on the international rules of the road (chapter seven) and on automobile associations throughout the word (chapter 13). State by state and province by province rules of the road for studs on tires, radar detectors, insurance, headsets are included in chapters five and six, for ready reference when you need it.

Roadside emergency information is at your fingertips. Even if you have never changed a tire, in chapter 18 an experienced auto mechanic explains step-by-step how to change a tire safely. First aid is also explained in an easy to understand manner, by an orthopaedic surgeon. If you are involved in an accident, you get a lawyer's advice on what to do and what not to do.

By keeping the *Glove Compartment Book* in your car you are keeping a mechanic, doctor and a lawyer available when you need them.

Part One
Driver's Legal
Manual

Chapter Two: Insurance

Whenever you drive one of the most important things to check before you start the engine, is to make sure that your insurance covers you. For example, most American insurance companies automatically insure you when you drive into Canada, but it makes sense to double-check this before you leave home. (If you are traveling to Canada you first should get an Interprovincial Financial Reponsibility Card from your insurance company. See chapter six on driving in Canada.) Similarly, most American insurance policies provide coverage for short trips into Mexico (usually 25 miles or less). For longer trips into Mexico you will have to purchase extra coverage at the border.

Always bring proof of insurance with you. Your insurance company will give you an insurance "binder," which is basically a receipt showing insurance coverage. Most states in the United States require drives to produce proof of financial responsibility if they are in an accident. This means that you must prove either that you are insured, or have sufficient assets, to cover the damage that you have caused. Write down your insurance information below:

Insurance Company:_____

Policy Number:_____

Agent's Name:_____

Agent's Telephone No.:_____

Limits of Coverage:_____

Insurance is mandatory in Europe and your green insurance card will often be checked at the border. If you are buying a car in Europe make sure that you have insurance effective when you pick up the vehicle. Be able to prove that you have insurance coverage if you are stopped by police, or are asked at the border.

Insurance Terminology

Your insurance agent may have sold you a $25,000/$50,000/$10,000 policy. What does this mean? First of all those figures are concerned with **liability** coverage. **Liability insurance** means that you are insured for damage that you cause to others. The first amount listed is the maximum amount that you insurance company will pay for personal injury caused to one person. The second figure is the amount of coverage that you have for one accident. If two persons are injured, the above policy will pay up to $25,000 for each of the two victims. The last figure is the amount of property damage coverage. This coverage will pay for damage to another person's car, or to a building that you have damaged.

For most people a $25,000/$50,000/$10,000 policy is **not** adequate. If you cause serious injury or death, you may be liable for $1 million or more. And if you own a home or have other substantial property, and your insurance is inadequate, you may lose your home or business. I personally have $300,000/$500,000/$50,000 coverage and will raise it to $500,000/$1 million. I recommend that you buy as much coverage as you can afford. If you have a substantial amount of property, you should have a substantial amount of automobile insurance. To protect themselves from major catastrophes, including auto accidents, many people have **umbrella** policies. An **umbrella** policy will increase all of your insurance coverage, including your auto and homeowner's policies, but will only pay claims if your individual policy limits are exceeded. For example, if you have a $250,000/$500,000 liability policy, and an accident victim wins a judgment against you for $300,000, your policy will only pay $250,000 to that one victim. However, if you had an umbrella policy for a million dollars, the umbrella policy will cover the $50,000 balance. Umbrella policies are inexpensive, because large settlements are rare. Rates for this coverage is based on the limits of your other policies.

Collision coverage is insurance for damage that you cause to your own car. If you car is a clunker, you can delete this coverage. Otherwise, I recommend getting a high deductible. This will substantially reduce your insurance premium. A deductible of $250.00 means that if you cause damage to your own vehicle you must pay the first $250.00. The insurance company will pay the rest.

Uninsured Motorist insurance is mandatory in many states, but often only for $20,000/$40,000/$10,000 or even less. This insurance will pay for your damages when an uninsured motorist causes damage to your car or person. Your uninsured coverage should be just as high as your liability protection. You buy insurance to protect yourself, and that is what uninsured motorist coverage is for. Make sure that your policy also covers **underinsured** motorists. For example, if you are hit by someone who has very little insurance, your policy may not pay you for additional harm that you have suffered. The fine print of the policy may only provide for payments in cases where the other driver is uninsured, not underinsured.

Agreed value insurance specifies in advance the amount that you will be paid if your car is totalled. Ordinarily an insurance company will only pay you the "blue book" value of your car when it is totally destroyed. However, if you keep your car in excellent condition, or if it is a classic car, you should ask for "agreed value" protection. This protection costs very little, but could mean a great deal if your car is badly damaged.

No-fault insurance. The insurance policies discussed so far were for states where motorists who are at-fault in causing an accident are required to pay for damage caused to innocent parties. In an increasing number of states this rule is being changed to a **no-fault** or modified no-fault system. While no-fault systems vary, they generally provide that each drive insures himself (or herself) and passengers in his car. Most liability insurance companies will provide no-fault coverage when you drive into a no-fault state. Before taking a trip, ask your insurance agent if you are covered in the states where you are going. If you plan to be in another state for more than thirty-days, you may be required to purchase no-fault insurance in that state. Again, check with your insurance agent, or call the Superintendent of Insurance in the state where you are planning to spend a month or more. In chapter five a list of states with no-fault insurance, or other compulsory insurance, is listed. However, as this area of the law is changing rapidly, you should check before taking an extended trip.

Chapter Three:
U.S. Road Signs

Regulatory Signs

STOP

YIELD

DO NOT
ENTER

NO LEFT
TURN

NO RIGHT
TURN

NO U
TURN

RIGHT TURN
ONLY

LEFT TURN
ONLY

LEFT OR
THROUGH

RIGHT OR
THROUGH

KEEP
RIGHT

KEEP
LEFT

2-WAY LEFT
TURN LANE

RESTRICTED
LANE

NO TRUCKS

NO
HITCHHIKING

NO
BICYCLES

NO
PEDESTRIANS

MUST EXIT
LANE

ONE WAY
TRAFFIC

TRUCK
WEIGHT
LIMIT

NO PASSING
ZONE

DIVIDED
HIGHWAY

NO
PARKING

RESERVED
PARKING FOR
HANDICAPPED

BUS STOP

TOW AWAY
ZONE

Warning Signs

RIGHT
TURN

LEFT
TURN

RIGHT
CURVE

LEFT
CURVE

RIGHT
REVERSE
TURN

LEFT
REVERSE
TURN

RIGHT
REVERSE
CURVE

LEFT
REVERSE
CURVE

WINDING
ROAD (RIGHT)

WINDING
ROAD (LEFT)

SHARP
CURVE TO
LEFT

ROADWAY
ALIGNMENT

CROSS
ROAD

SIDE
ROAD
(LEFT)

SIDE
ROAD
(RIGHT)

SIDE
ROAD

Y
INTERSECTION

T
INTERSECTION

12

STOP
AHEAD

YIELD
AHEAD

SIGNAL
AHEAD

MERGING
TRAFFIC
(FROM RIGHT)

ADDED LANE
(FROM RIGHT)

TWO WAY
TRAFFIC

FIRE
STATION

ROAD
NARROWS
(FROM RIGHT)

HILL

DIVIDED
HIGHWAY

DIVIDED
HIGHWAY
ENDS

SLIPPERY
WHEN WET

HANDICAPPED CROSSING

PLAYGROUND

LOW VERTICAL CLEARANCE

NARROW BRIDGE

PAVEMENT ENDS

TRUCK CROSSING

SNOWMOBILE CROSSING

EQUESTRIAN CROSSING

FARM MACHINERY CROSSING

CATTLE CROSSING

DEER CROSSING

PEDESTRIAN CROSSING

BIKE
CROSSING

SCHOOL
ZONE

SCHOOL
CROSSING

LOW
SHOULDER

WORKERS
AHEAD

FLAGGER
AHEAD

DETOUR

HILL
(BICYCLE)

RAILROAD
CROSSING

RAILROAD
ADVANCE
CROSSING

Service Signs

GAS

DIESEL

MECHANIC

LODGING

FOOD

PHONE

HOSPITAL

INFORMATION

FIRST AID

CAMPING
(TRAILER)

CAMPING
(TENT)

TRAILER
SANITARY
STATION

Chapter Four:
International Road Signs
Prohibitory or Regulatory Signs

YIELD

STOP

PRIORITY
ROAD

END OF
PRIORITY
ROAD

ONCOMING
TRAFFIC
HAS PRIORITY

PRIORITY OVER
ONCOMING
TRAFFIC

NO ENTRY

CLOSED TO
ALL VEHICLES

NO ENTRY
FOR CARS

NO ENTRY
MOTORCYCLES

NO ENTRY
BICYCLES

NO ENTRY FOR
POWERED
VEHICLES

NO ENTRY FOR
WIDE VEHICLES

NO ENTRY FOR
HIGH VEHICLES

NO ENTRY FOR
HEAVY VEHICLES

MAINTAIN DISTANCE BETWEEN VEHICLES

NO LEFT TURN

NO U-TURNS

TRAFFIC CIRCLE

NO PASSING

NO TRUCK PASSING

SPEED LIMIT

NO HORNS

STOP

END OF NO PASSING ZONE

END OF SPEED LIMIT

MINIMUM SPEED

END OF MINIMUM SPEED

DIRECTION TO BE FOLLOWED

PASS THIS SIDE

SNOW CHAINS MANDATORY

END OF LOCAL PROHIBITIONS

Danger Warning Signs

RIGHT CURVE

DOUBLE CURVE

DANGEROUS CURVE

DANGEROUS DESCENT

STEEP ASCENT

PEDESTRIAN CROSSING

ROADWAY NARROWS

DRAW BRIDGE

ROAD LEADS TO RIVER OR LAKE

BUMPS

BUMP

DIP

SLIPPERY

LOOSE GRAVEL

FALLING ROCKS

CHILDREN

CYCLISTS

CATTLE CROSSING

DEER CROSSING

ROAD WORK

SIGNAL

CROSS-WIND

TWO-WAY TRAFFIC

DANGER!

INTERSECTION   INTERSECTION WITH ROAD WHICH MUST YIELD   TRAFFIC CIRCLE

   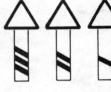

RAILROAD CROSSING   TROLLEY CROSSING

APPROACHES TO LEVEL CROSSING

Informative Signs

ONE WAY ROAD   NO THROUGH ROAD   DIVIDED HIGHWAY   END OF DIVIDED HIGHWAY

ROAD FOR MOTOR VEHICLES   END OF ROAD FOR MOTOR VEHICLES   BUS STOP   TROLLEY STOP

DETOUR

ROUTE

TURNS PERMITTED

PRIORITY ROAD

BEGINNING OF CITY

END OF CITY

NO THROUGH ROAD

HOSPITAL

Standing & Parking Signs

ALTERNATE
PARKING

LIMITED PARKING

NO PARKING

NO STANDING
OR PARKING

PARKING ON ODD
NUMBER DATES
PROHIBITED

PARKING ON EVEN
NUMBER DATES
PROHIBITED

PARKING

END OF NO
PARKING ZONE

Service Signs

TOURIST INFORMATION

FIRST-AID STATION

SERVICE STATION

TELEPHONE

GASOLINE STATION

HOTEL

RESTAURANT

SNACK BAR

PICNIC SITE

HIKING

CAMPING

TRAILERS

CAMPING AND TRAILERS

YOUTH HOSTEL

Miscellaneous Signs

AUSTRIA

TRAM TURNS AT YELLOW OR RED

DETOUR

BUSES ONLY

U-TURN ONLY

22

FEDERAL ROAD WITH PRIORITY   FEDERAL ROAD WITHOUT PRIORITY

BELGIUM

DANGEROUS AREA   TURN LEFT OR RIGHT   NO PARKING FROM 1ST TO 15TH OF MONTH   NO PARKING FROM 16TH TO END OF MONTH

BULGARIA

ROAD FOR PRIVATE CARS   U-TURN ALLOWED   RECOMMENDED MAXIMUM SPEED   NO TRUCK LANE

DENMARK

PASS EITHER SIDE   RECOMMENDED SAFE SPEED   TRAFFIC MERGES   COMPULSORY SLOW LANE   SIGHT-SEEING

FRANCE

PRIORITY OVER OTHER ROAD   DANGEROUS INTERSECTION-YIELD TO TRAFFIC FROM RIGHT   END OF PARKING PROHIBITION

23

NO PARKING 1ST TO 15TH OF MONTH NO PARKING 16TH TO END OF MONTH PARKING ON ALTERNATE SIDES BUS LANE END OF BUS LANE

KEEP RIGHT FLAMMABLE FOREST HOLIDAY ROUTE ALTERNATIVE ROUTE

GERMAN DEMOCRATIC REPUBLIC

SLOW LANE 2 HOUR PARKING WITH PARKING STICKER TRANSIT ROUTE DANGER—FOG

GERMANY (Federal Republic)

BUS OR TROLLEY STOP RECOMMENDED SPEED RANGE DETOUR EMERGENCY DETOUR

24

HUNGARY

DETOUR

TRUCK ROUTE

BUS LANE

ITALY

NO PARKING

NO PASSING
FOR TRAILERS

STOP WHEN
MEETING BUS ON
MOUNTAIN ROADS

FLAMMABLE
FOREST

CYCLE PATH

AUTO ROAD

TRAFFIC IN
TWO LANES

SLOW LANE

SNOW TIRES OR
CHAINS REQUIRED

NETHERLANDS

B ROAD

End of B road

CYCLE PATH
(NO MOPEDS)

CYCLISTS
CROSSING

END OF CITY

25

NORWAY

PARKING PERMITTED
FOR 2 HOURS
BETWEEN STATED TIMES

PARKING PERMITTED
FOR 2 HOURS
(SATURDAY HOURS)

STOPPING OR PARKING
PROHIBITED FROM 8–10 AM
PERMITTED FROM
10 AM TO 5 PM
(SATURDAY UNTIL 3 PM)

SIGHT-SEEING PASSING PLACE TUNNEL

ROAD MERGES

SPAIN

TAKE CARE

SIGHT-SEEING

TOURIST
OFFICE

TURNING
PERMITTED

RECOMMENDED
MAXIMUM
SPEED

NO ENTRY

COMPULSORY
LANE FOR
MOTORCYCLES

COMPULSORY
LANE FOR TRUCKS

FLAMMABLE
FOREST

SWEDEN

TUNNEL

PASSING PLACE

SWITZERLAND

PASSING PLACE

SLOW LANE

FLASHING LIGHTS
AT RR CROSSING

PARKING STICKER
NEEDED

TRAILERS
PROHIBITED

MOUNTAIN
POSTAL ROAD

TUNNEL
(LIGHTS ON)

SEMI-DIVIDED
HIGHWAY

BUS LANE

UNITED KINGDOM

RING ROAD
(BELTWAY)

NO STOPPING

NATIONAL
SPEED
LIMIT

CONTRA-FLOW
BUS LANE

TRUCK ROUTE

Chapter Five: Rules of the Road for the United States

by Edward F. Kearney, former Executive Director, National Committee on Uniform Traffic Laws & Ordinances

Introduction

Rules of the road tell people how to drive or walk on the highways. They apply to all forms of traffic, including motor vehicles, pedestrians, bicycles and persons riding or driving animals. When everyone follows these rules, traffic moves safely and efficiently. When the rules are disobeyed, the possibility of a crash is significantly increased. Most crashes are caused by violating these rules.

Under the traffic laws of most states, violating a rule of the road is a crime called a misdemeanor punishable by a fine or jail sentence, or both. Repeated violations carry higher penalties than first violations and can result in loss of a person's driving privileges.

Essential rules of the road are adopted by the legislature in each state. Most state rules are patterned after the *Uniform Vehicle Code,* which is a guide for the states to use to make their laws meaningful in terms of today's traffic, and to make them uniform with the laws of other states.

Above and beyond all rules of the road, however, is the need to remember at all times that your safety, and the safety of others, depends largely on your own safe, alert driving habits. Sensible driving includes avoiding a collision with persons who disregard the rules stated in this Chapter. Always expect the unexpected; be prepared for people who do not follow the rules described in this Chapter.

Police Officers

Drivers, pedestrians and other users of the highway must comply with the instructions of a police officer who is regulating traffic.

In a green light indicates that you may proceed, but a police officer signals you to stop, you must stop. If a red light indicates that you must stop but a police officer signals you to go, you should go.

Traffic Control Devices

Drivers must comply with the instructions of traffic control devices. Such devices include signs, signals and pavement markings that have been installed for the purpose of regulating, warning or guiding traffic.

Traffic control devices include stop signs, yield signs, speed limit signs, steady and flashing red signals, yellow center lines and white lane lines.

Starting a Stopped Vehicle

Move a stopped vehicle only when you are certain it is safe to proceed.

Always look to the rear to determine whether any pedestrians or vehicles are there before backing a vehicle. An alert driver asseses the situation to the rear of the vehicle before he enters it; and again before moving.

Speed

One of the most important rules of the road is called the "basic speed rule." It requires drives at all times to drive at a speed that is reasonable and prudent for existing conditions, considering potential as well as existing hazards. This rule requires driving at a safe and appropriate speed near intersections, railroad grade crossings, curves, hills, and on narrow or winding roads. Also, you should reduce your speed when special hazards exist because of traffic or weather conditions.

Thus, even though a law or a sign specifies a particular speed limit, a person should always drive at a lower rate of speed whenever conditions indicate that the lower speed is reasonable and prudent.

Subject to the "basic speed rule," specific speed limits for driving in urban and rural areas are set by state law. Usually speed limits will be indicated by a sign. It is unlawful to drive faster than the speed limit specified in a state law or one that is indicated by a sign. And remember, even though a law or a sign specifies a maximum speed limit of 55 mph (approximately 90 kilometers per hour), the basic speed rule requires a lower speed whenever conditions indicate that the lower speed would be reasonable and prudent. The maximum speed limit in the United States is currently 55 miles per hour (90 kph).

On the other hand, a person should never proceed at such a slow speed as to impede the normal and reasonable movement of traffic—except when the slow speed becomes necessary for safe operation or to comply with other rules of the road. Minimum limits are set for some highways, and when a minimum speed sign is posted it is unlawful to drive at a slower speed except, as already explained, when it is necessary for safe operation or to comply with other rules of the road, including the "basic speed rule." In other words, if a sign indicates that the minimum speed is 40 mph, a drive must drive at least that fast unless conditions indicate that a slower speed is reasonable and prudent.

Drive on the Right Side of the Roadway

In the United States and most other nations, drivers must stay on the right half of any roadway on which traffic moves in opposite directions. Six exceptions to this general rule have been made to allow driving on the left side of a two-way roadway:

1. When instructed to do so by a police officer;
2. When permitted to do so by a traffic-control sign, signal or marking;
3. When driving across the highway to make a left turn;
4. When lawfully using the middle lane of a roadway with an odd number of lanes;
5. When driving around an obstruction; or
6. When passing a vehicle proceeding in the same direction.

Rules for Passing. When passing another vehicle a driver must not interfere with the safe operation of that vehicle. The driver must keep a safe distance away from the other vehicle and should not return to the original lane of travel until safely clear of the overtaken vehicle.

When passing a vehicle by driving on the left side of a two-way roadway, a drive must not interfere with the operation of a vehicle approaching from the opposite direction.

A drive may not pass another vehicle by driving on the left side of a two-way roadway:

1. If the roadway has four or more lanes;
2. When the vehicles are within 100 feet of or crossing any intersection or railroad grade crossing;
3. When the vehicles are approaching or on a curve or hill where the driver cannot see far enough ahead to be certain that no other vehicle is approaching from the opposite direction; or
4. In a no-passing zone indicated by a sign or marking.

If you are driving a vehicle about to be passed, you must not increase your speed until the overtaking vehicle has passed you.

Driving Around an Obstruction. A driver can use the left side of a two-way roadway when necessary to drive around an obstruction, such as a ditch or a disabled vehicle. However, you must yield the right of way to vehicles traveling in the opposite direction on the unobstructed part of the roadway.

Middle Lane. When traffic is moving in two directions and there are three or five lanes on the roadway, the middle lane may be used in several different ways. There may be signs, signals or markings indicating your direction, or only by vehicles proceeding in the opposite direction. Some center lanes in urban areas are designated for use by drivers proceeding in both directions, but only for the purpose of making a left turn. In the absence of any indications, the center lane must be used only to make a left turn or to pass another vehicle if the lane is free of oncoming vehicles though three-lane roadways are becoming increasingly rare.

Passing on the Right

When the roadway is unobstructed and is wide enough for at least two lines of vehicles moving in the same direction, a driver may pass on the right side of another vehicle. Passing on the right is permitted only when safe. A driver passing on the right may not drive off the roadway, and may not use the shoulder even if it is paved.

Driving on Laned Roadways

When a roadway has clearly marked lanes, a vehicle must stay within a single lane as much as possible, safe and reasonable.

Changing lanes is prohibited unless and until it is safe to do so. All lane changes must be preceded by an adequate turn signal indicating your intention to move right or left on the roadway. Turn signals are discussed in a subsequent part of this Chapter.

Selection of the Proper Lane

When there is more than one lane for traffic moving in the same direction, you are required to use any lane designated as appropriate for the type of vehicle you are driving or for the rate of speed at which you are proceeding. For example, you must use the right lane whenever the speed of your vehicle is less than the normal speed of traffic unless you are preparing for a left turn or passing. The sign often used to remind drivers of this rule reads: "Slower traffic keep right."

In addition to these rules, there are other factors to consider in choosing the lane in which to drive. Some of these factors are: your speed and the speed of other vehicles, the amount of traffic, the desirability of being as far away from vehicles proceeding in the opposite direction as possible, the necessity to turn off the highway to reach your destination, merging traffic, and your safety.

Traffic Moving in Opposite Directions

Where traffic moves in two directions, drivers proceeding in opposite directions must give each other at least one-half of the available roadway space when it is possible to do so. On all roadways, drivers proceeding in opposite directions pass each other by keeping to their right.

Right of Way Between Vehicles

Drivers Entering Highways. Drivers entering a roadway from any place other than another highway must yield the right of way to all vehicles on the roadway to be entered or crossed. This rule means that drivers emerging from driveways, private roads, buildings or land areas adjacent to a highway must yield the right of way to vehicles approaching on the highway.

Left Turns. A driver intending to make a left turn must yield the right of way to any vehicle approaching from the opposite direction.

This rule applies to drivers making a left turn at any location, including intersections and driveways. The driver's duty is to yield to any vehicle approaching from the opposite direction, including oncoming vehicles making a right turn and vehicles proceeding straight ahead.

Uncontrolled Intersections. When two vehicles approach or enter an intersection from different highways at approximately the same time, the driver of the vehicle on the left must yield the right of way to the vehicle on his right.

This rule does not apply when the driver of the vehicle on the right faces a red light, stop sign or yield sign. It also does not apply when the driver on the left is operating an ambulance or fire vehicle sounding a siren and displaying flashing red lights, a police vehicle sounding a siren, or a highway maintenance vehicle engaged in work on a highway displaying flashing yellow lights.

Stop Signs. A driver approaching a stop sign has two principal duties: stop and yield the right of way.

If you are on a roadway governed by a stop sign, you must stop at a stop line or at a place indicated by a special sign. If there is no such line or sign, you should stop before entering the crosswalk. If there is no line, sign or crosswalk, the stop should be made at the point nearest the intersecting roadway where you will have a clear view of approaching traffic.

After stopping, you must yield the right of way to any vehicle in the intersection or approaching on another roadway so closely as to constitute a hazard during the time you are moving across or within the intersection or junction of roadways. It is thus quite apparent that drivers at stop signs may have to stop more than once before crossing an intersection governed by a stop sign.

Yield Signs. A driver approaching a yield sign must slow and yield the right of way. If necessary for safety, a stop must be made at the appropriate place as specified in preceding paragraphs for stop signs—at the stop line, sign or crosswalk, or if there are none of these at a point near the intersecting roadway where you have a clear view of traffic on the intersecting roadway.

After slowing or stopping for a yield sign, a driver must yield the right of way to any vehicle that is in the intersection or so near to it on another roadway as to constitute a hazard during the time such driver is moving across or within the intersection.

Authorized Emergency Vehicles. Drivers must yield the right of way to any authorized emergency vehicle, such as a police vehicle, fire truck or ambulance. This requirement to yield applies only when the emergency vehicle is sounding a special audible signal (such as a siren) and displaying special flashing or rotating lights (red or blue). However, many states do not require police vehicles to display special flashing lights. Drivers of these emergency vehicles are authorized to ignore stop signs and red lights and you must yield to them when they do. If the emergency vehicle approaches you from the rear, you should slow down, pull over and stop when it is possible and safe to do so.

Highway Construction and Maintenance Vehicles. Drivers must yield the right of way to vehicles engaged in work on the highway when those vehicles are displaying special flashing or rotating yellow lights.

Drivers must also yield to vehicles engaged in work on a highway within a construction area that is indicated by official traffic-control devices.

Pedestrians

A driver's most important legal duty with respect to any pedestrian is to avoid hitting him or her.

In addition, a driver must yield the right of way to a pedestrian crossing a roadway in any marked crosswalk or in any unmarked crosswalk at an intersection, to any pedestrian on a sidewalk, to any pedestrian working in a construction area designated by traffic-control devices, and to any blind pedestrian carrying a clearly visible white cane or accompanied by a guide dog.

A driver must not pass a vehicle stopped at a crosswalk to allow a pedestrian to cross.

Though pedestrians crossing a roadway outside a crosswalk generally are required to yield to vehicular traffic, your legal duty as a driver is to exercise care to avoid a collision.

Traffic Control Signals

Commonly used at intersections a traffic-control signal is an electrical device by which traffic is alternately directed to stop and permitted to proceed. Traffic control signals use only green, yellow and red lights.

Circular green means that drivers facing the indication may proceed but must yield the right of way to pedestrians in adjacent crosswalks and to all traffic within the intersection. In most states, a circular green means a driver may proceed straight ahead or turn right or left unless otherwise indicated by a sign.

Green arrow means that drivers may enter the intersection to make the movement indicated by the green arrow but they must yield to pedestrians in adjacent crosswalks and to all traffic within the intersection.

Circular yellow or yellow arrow warns that a red indication will soon be exhibited or that the related green signal is being terminated. Thus, it is lawful to enter an intersection on a yellow light. (May older drivers are instructed under earlier laws to stop for a yellow light unless it would be unsafe to do so.)

The decision to stop or go when facing a circular yellow light is a complicated one involving many factors, such as:

1. The number of seconds the yellow signal has been displayed.

2. Your speed and distance from the intersection.

3. Whether you can see traffic on the intersecting street and, if so, what it is doing.

4. The proximity of vehicles following you.

5. Condition of the road surface.

6. The presence of pedestrians and other vehicles on or near your roadway.

Circular red means that a driver must stop before reaching a stop line. If there is no line, a driver must stop before entering the crosswalk. If there is no stop line or crosswalk, the stop must be made before entering the intersection.

A driver must remain stopped until an indication to proceed is shown. An indication to proceed could be a green light or a flashing yellow signal.

However, **a driver may make a right turn on a red light** after stopping and yielding the right of way to pedestrians in adjacent crosswalks and to all traffic using the intersection **unless a sign prohibits the turn.** They may also turn left on red from a one-way street into another one-way street. All drivers proceeding on a green signal should anticipate drivers turning right on red from intersecting streets.

Steady red arrow means that drivers may not enter the intersection to proceed in the direction in which the arrow is pointing. It is usually used following a green arrow and a yellow arrow. Drivers wishing to proceed in the direction indicated by the arrow must stop before a stop line or crosswalk or, if none, before entering the intersection. As to a red arrow pointing to the right, may a driver make a right turn after stopping and yielding in your state?

If a traffic-control signal is used at a non-intersection location, the meanings described above for a green, yellow or red signal apply insofar as they can. Any required stop must be made at a sign or line or, if none, then at the signal.

Flashing Signals

Flashing yellow means that drivers should proceed with caution.

Flashing red means the same thing as a stop sign. A driver must stop and yield the right of way.

Some people do not know that a flashing red light means stop and yield the right of way. So if you approach an intersection and see a flashing yellow light, be prepared to stop for drivers approaching a flashing red on an intersecting highway.

Pedestrians and Signals

Pedestrians may cross the roadway on a "Walk" signal and drivers must yield the right of way to them. Pedestrians should not begin to cross the street when a "Don't Walk" signal is displayed but may complete a crossing begun during a "Walk" interval.

Pedestrians are not supposed to cross a roadway against a steady red or yellow signal unless a "Walk" signal is shown. Pedestrians may cross on a circular green or green straight through arrow unless prohibited by a "Don't Walk." They are not supposed to cross when the only green signal is a turn arrow, unless allowed by a "Walk" signal.

Pedestrians are not required to comply with flashing yellow or flashing red lights.

Again, a driver's paramount legal responsibility is to avoid hitting any pedestrian even if the pedestrian is violating a law.

Lane—Direction—Control Signals

When special lane-control signals have been placed over individual lanes on a highway, a driver may travel in any lane over which a green signal is shown but must not enter or travel in any lane over which a red signal is shown. Such signals are usually in the form of a green arrow pointing straight down and a red X.

If the lane signal is a steady yellow one, be prepared to leave that lane when a red signal is shown. Usually this signal will be steady yellow X.

A flashing yellow lane signal designates a lane to be used to make a left turn. Usually this will be a flashing yellow X.

Turning Movements

A driver before turning must first ascertain whether it is safe to turn and must give an adequate advance signal of his intention to turn. Turns at intersections and some other locations must also follow prescribed courses.

Safety. A person should never turn from a direct course of move right or left on the roadway when it would create a hazard for another driver. the laws of all states require a driver who turns or changes lanes to make reasonably certain that his movement will be safe.

Signal. One must give a signal before turning from a direct course or before moving right or left on the roadway. For instance, a turn signal is required before changing lanes, leaving one roadway to enter another, leaving the highway to enter any adjacent land area and, or course, before turning at an intersection.

A signal of intention to turn or move laterally on the roadway must be given for at least the last 100 feet traveled before turning. When turning from a parked position or when changing lanes at speeds in excess of 50 miles per hour, the turn signal should be given for three to five seconds before turning.

A turn signal may be given either by hand and arm or by electric turn signal lamps that have been installed on most motor vehicles. These lamps flash on the left side to indicate a left turn and on the right side to indicate a right turn. Most vehicles have turn signals on the front and rear. Drivers generally use the electric turn signal indicators because they are more convenient than giving a hand-and-arm signal and because they usually are more visible to other drivers. There may, however, be situations when a hand-and-arm signal may be necessary as, for instance, when the electric signal is not functioning or when the vehicle is not equipped with them. It may also be desirable to give a hand signal before pulling out of a line of parked cars or to supplement the electric signal.

Hand-and-arm signals are given from the left side of the vehicle. To signal a left turn, your hand and arm should be extended horizontally. To signal a right turn, the hand and arm should be extended upward.

Proper Position and Courses for Turns. Unless otherwise indicated by traffic-control devices, a driver intending to turn right should approach and make the turn as near as practicable to the right-hand curb or edge of the roadway.

The approach for a left turn should be made in the extreme left lane available for traffic moving in your direction. If there is a special lane designated for left turns, it should be used. Whenever possible and safe, the turn itself should be made to the left of the center of an intersection and in such a manner that the vehicle will leave the intersection in the extreme left lane available to traffic moving in that direction.

U—Turns. A driver may not turn so as to proceed in the opposite direction unless this movement can be made in safety and without interfering with other traffic. Such turns are prohibited on curves and hills where the turning vehicle cannot be seen for 500 feet in each direction. It is recommended that you never make a U or Y turn in a no-passing zone where the speed limit is more than 35 miles per hour.

You should never make any turn prohibited by a sign, signal, or other traffic-control device.

Left Turns and Yellow Lines. Though it is lawful to make a left turn across two solid parallel yellow lines, a driver should be particularly careful in making such a turn either for the purpose of entering the highway or leaving it. Double solid yellow lines are often used to indicate or a no passing zone where hills or curves prevent an adequate view of approaching vehicles.

If a highway has been divided into two roadways by the installation of yellow lines to outline a paved, uncurbed median, it is lawful to make a left turn across the median unless any such turn has been prohibited by a sign. If you must wait for oncoming vehicles before turning, pull into the median area so your car will not obstruct traffic if it is wide enough. You may not drive into nor across an unpaved median on a divided highway.

Serious Traffic Offenses

All rules of the road are important. Violating any rule described in this Chapter can and does cause death, injury or delay. Nonetheless, there is a special category of rules in state vehicle codes prohibiting particularly dangerous behavior. The types of improper behavior described in this section so dramatically increase the likelihood of crashes and injuries that most states prescribe much more severe penalties for violating them in comparison with violations of other rules of the road.

Racing. It is unlawful on a highway to engage in a race, drag race, speed competition, acceleration contest, or exhibition of speed or acceleration. Under the *Uniform Vehicle Code,* the penalty for violating this rule is a maximum fine of $500 and/or imprisonment for six months. Further, the department of motor vehicles may suspend the convicted person's driver's license. In one or two states, a vehicle used in a race can be confiscated and sold, with the proceeds from its sale becoming the property of the state.

Eluding a Police Officer. A driver should not flee from or try to elude a pursuing marked police car after having received a visual or audible signal to stop form a uniformed police officer. The penalty for violating this rule under the *Uniform Vehicle Code* is at least $100 fine and/or 30 days in jail and can be up to $500 and/or six months in jail. License suspension is authorized.

Reckless Driving. You should never drive in willful or wanton disregard for the safety or persons or property. The penalty for reckless driving in the *Uniform Vehicle Code* is five to 90 days in jail and/or a fine of $25 to $500.

Alcohol. It is unlawful for a person to drive a vehicle while under the influence of alcohol. This means that a person should not drive when his mental or physical ability to drive safely has been impaired by alcohol. Upon conviction of this offense under the *Uniform Vehicle Code*, the minimum penalty is 10 days in jail or a fine of $100 and the maximum penalty is one year in jail or $1,000. A second conviction of drunk driving under the *Code* requires the person to spend three months in jail and, in addition, a fine of $1,000 may be imposed.

An increasing number of states are adopting laws authorizing special medical or other treatment of convicted drunk drivers on the basis that they may suffer an illness which requires care rather than punishment.

Another new trend in state laws is to make it unlawful for a person to drive with more than a specified amount of alcohol in his blood, usually 10/100ths of one percent.

Because of its seriousness and known relation to accident causation, conviction of drunk driving will also result in loss of one's driving privileges.

Drugs. No person should drive while under the influence of any drug to a degree which renders him incapable of driving safely. The penalties in the *Uniform Vehicle Code* for drugged driving are the same as those for drunk driving.

Homicide by Vehicle. It is unlawful to violate a rule of the road and in so doing to unintentionally cause another person to die. The penalty under the *Uniform Vehicle Code* is one to five years in the state penitentiary or three months to one year in the county jail and/or a fine of $500 to $2,000. A person convicted of this serious offense will also lose his driving privileges. In some states, this offense is called "manslaughter by motor vehicle." An intentional killing of another person by using a motor vehicle (i.e., murder by car) is beyond the scope of this book and would carry much higher penalties.

Stopping, Standing and Parking

Never stop on the roadway when it is safe to stop off the roadway, particularly outside urban areas. This rule does not apply to stops that may be necessary to avoid conflict with other traffic or to comply with the directions of a police officer or traffic-control device.

You also should not stop your vehicle at the following places:

1. Within an intersection or on railroad tracks.
2. On a crosswalk.
3. On a sidewalk.
4. On the roadway side of a vehicle stopped or parked at the curb or edge of a street (i.e., "double-parking").
5. On a bridge or in a tunnel.
6. In a median strip between roadways.
7. On a controlled-access highway, including interstate highways.
8. At any place where a sign prohibits stopping.

It is all right to stop at the above places when necessary to avoid a collision and to comply with the directions of an officer or a traffic-control device.

Signs and regulations frequently prohibit "standing" or "parking" within certain distances of fire hydrants, crosswalks and stop signs. Stopping in such areas is generally prohibited except to load or unload persons or property. The only difference between a "No standing" and a "no parking" restriction deals with unloading property. If a sign bans parking, you may stop temporarily to load or unload passengers or property. If a sign prohibits standing, you may stop momentarily only to receive or discharge passengers. In other words, loading or unloading property in a no standing zone is prohibited. Though stops in no parking zones are generally prohibited, the restrictions do not apply to the necessary or unavoidable stops of the type previously discussed in conjunction with stopping restrictions.

When parking on any street or roadway where traffic moves in two directions, the right wheels of your vehicle must be within 12 inches of the right curb or as close to the right edge of the right shoulder as possible. Parking on the wrong side of the street is illegal. On a one-way roadway, you must park with the right wheels within 12 inches of the right curb or the left wheels within 12 inches of the left curb. If there are no curbs, park as far off the roadway on the shoulder as is reasonable and safe.

Traffic control devices may be installed to modify these rules or to remind drives of their existence.

These rules do not apply when your vehicle is disabled and it is impossible to avoid temporarily violating them. In such cases, every effort should be made to place the vehicle off the roadway on the shoulder and you must arrange to have the vehicle removed, serviced or repaired as soon as possible.

Miscellaneous Driving Rules

Following Too Closely. A driver should not follow another vehicle more closely than is reasonable and prudent. In deciding how far to remain away from the vehicle in front of you, consideration should be given to all pertinent traffic conditions including the speed of your vehicle and the one in front of you.

Stops at Railroad Grade Crossings. You must stop at railroad grade crossings when:

1. A stop sign has been erected.

2. An electric or mechanical signal warns of the approach of a train. These usually consist of flashing red lights or bells.

3. A crossing gate is lowered. It is illegal to drive past a gate that is closed or being opened or closed.

4. A flagman warns of the approach of a train.

5. An approaching train is planing visible or emits an audible signal within 1,500 feet and is in hazardous proximity to the crossing.

The stop must be made from 15 to 50 feet away from the nearest rail. You may proceed when it is safe to do so.

Drivers of school buses and vehicles carrying certain hazardous materials such as gasoline or explosives are required to stop before crossing railroad tracks. If you are following such vehicles near railroad crossings, be prepared for their stop.

Stopping for School Bus. Under the *Uniform Vehicle Code,* drivers would stop for a school bus when four conditions exist:

1. The school bus is stopped.

2. The school bus is yellow in color.

3. The school bus displays signs stating "School Bus."

4. The school bus is displaying special, alternately flashing red lights.

Because of the large number of differences in state laws in this area, however, you should find out of specific rule in effect in your state. You must remain stopped until the school bus resumes motion or until the special flashing red lights are turned off. You are not required to stop for a school bus that is on a different roadway of a divided highway.

Emerging Driver to Stop. In urban areas, drivers emerging from alleys, buildings, driveways and private roads must stop before driving onto any sidewalk. If there is no sidewalk, the stop should be made at a point where the driver has a view of approaching traffic.

As previously noted, drivers emerging from such places must yield the right of way to pedestrians on sidewalks and to vehicles approaching on the roadway to be entered.

Backing. Make certain it is safe to back your vehicle. You may never drive backward on a controlled-access highway.

Unattended Vehicle. Before leaving a motor vehicle unattended, you must:

1. Stop the engine.
2. Lock the ignition.
3. Remove the key from the ignition.
4. Set the parking brake.
5. Turn the front wheels to the side or curb if the vehicle is on a hill.

It is also advisable to lock the doors and close the windows in many urban areas to protect your car and its contents from theft.

Driving on Sidewalk. Motor vehicles should not be operated on sidewalks except to cross them in driveways or alleys.

Opening Door. Before opening any door on the side of the vehicle toward moving traffic, make certain you will not interfere with traffic. Don't leave the door open any longer than necessary. Watch out for passing bicyclists.

Following Fire Truck. You should not follow within 500 feet of fire truck traveling in response to a fire alarm. You also should not park within 500 feet of a fire truck stopped at a fire.

Obstructed Intersection. You should not enter an intersection when traffic on the other side is so congested that you cannot clear the intersection. This rule applies even though a green light indicates that you may proceed. You also should not drive on a railroad crossing when traffic on the other side is so congested as to require stopping on the crossing.

Entering/Leaving Controlled Access Highway. A vehicle may be driven from or onto a controlled access highway only at established entrances and exits.

Divided Highway. When a highway has been divided into two or more roadways, you must drive on the right-hand roadway unless use of a different one is permitted or directed a traffic-control device. Thus, the median will be on your left as a general rule. If the median is on your right, make certain you are not driving the "wrong way."

You may not drive in an unpaved area between two roadways. You may use a crossover between two roadways on a divided highway unless such use is prohibited by a traffic control device.

Number of People in Front Seat. When there are more than three people in the front seat of a vehicle and the drivers' view is obstructed or his control is hindered by such people, it is illegal to drive. You also may not drive a vehicle when it is so loaded that your view or control is hindered.

Coasting. You should not coast downhill with the gears or transmission in neutral.

Play Streets. When a sign indicates that a street has been designated a "play street," vehicles are banned unless their drivers live or have business there. Any such driver must exercise the greatest care.

Bicycles

Persons riding bicycles have the same rights and duties as other drivers. Because of bicyclists' vulnerability to injury, drivers should exercise every precaution to avoid colliding with them, particularly if they are small children.

Bicyclists are supposed to ride as near to the right side of roadway as is possible, safe and reasonable. Nonethless, bicyclists often must leave an area near the curb to pass parked cars, make left turns, keep out of a "Right Turn Only" lane and to avoid hazards not encountered by other drivers such as dangerous grates, glass, stones and rough pavement. Be very careful when passing bicycles.

Two bicycles may lawfully be ridden side by side in one lane of a roadway.

If there is a path or lane for bicycles, it should be used in preference to riding on the roadway.

If a "bike only" lane has been established in your community and is indicated by signs or markings on the roadway, drivers of motor vehicles must not travel in that lane although it may be crossed to enter or leave the street or to park. Such lanes are generally placed near the right side of city streets just inside spaces for parking. When turning at an intersection, drivers should be particularly careful as they cross the "bike only" lane.

Motorcycles

Although persons operating motorcycles have the same rights and responsibilities as the drivers of other vehicles, some special rules have been formulated for them.

A motorcyclists is entitled to use the full width of a traffic lane. The driver of another vehicle should never occupy space alongside a motorcycle in the same lane.

Motorcycles may be operated two abreast in the same lane.

Passengers may ride only on a seat or in a sidecar and only if the motorcycle is designed to carry more than one person. Riding "sidesaddle" is prohibited.

A collision between a car and a motorcycle usually results in injury to the motorcyclist because his vehicle affords no post-crash protection. Persons driving or riding motorcycles should wear helmets and approved eye protection devices.

Some states have laws requiring headlamps to be used by motorcycles during daylight hours in an effort to improve their visibility to drivers.

Equipment Rules

Head lamps. Head lamps and tail lamps must be lighted whenever you are driving at night, from one-half hour after sunset to one-half our before sunrise. They must also be used at any time when you cannot see persons and vehicles at a distance of 1,000 feet because of insufficient light or unfavorable atmospheric conditions.

Tires. Tires with no tread and tires with a tread depth under 1/16 of an inch are very dangerous and may not be lawfully used on the highways.

Horns. Horns should be used when reasonably necessary for safe driving. Any other use is illegal.

Brakes. Brakes are the most important operational system in any car. Every car is required by law to have brakes that will stop and hold it on level ground and on any hill where it is operated. Never drive a car with brakes that are not in good condition. You should have the brakes on your car inspected by a competent mechanic at least once each year.

State-by-State Differences*

Most states now require children to be in safety seats or seat belts. Only New York State and Puerto Rico require drivers and passengers to wear seat belts. I recommend that all passengers wear seat belts because they have proven to be effective in reducing injuries.

The following chart lists state laws on use of headsets, studded tires, radar detectors, AAA bailbond, and insurance. The chart lists insurance only if it is mandatory for liability (ML) or mandatory no-fault insurance (MNF). If a state requires judges and magistrates to accept the AAA bailbond card, the maximum amount that that state requires the AAA to be accepted for is listed. AAA bailbond cards are not accepted for drunk driving, driving without a valid license and a few other offenses. Judges and magistrates can permit use of the AAA bond card, even if not required to do so, or can allow it to be used for a higher amount. I recommend that drivers belong

---

*This section was prepared by the research staff of the National Press.

to the American Automobile Association because of their emergency road services, their map service and their bailbond card.

State	Studded Tires	Headsets	Radar Det.	Insurance	AAA Bail
Alabama	Metal Illegal	Legal	Legal		
Alaska	Sept 30–May 1 Until Apr 15 S of 60 Deg N	Illegal	Legal		
Arizona	Oct 1–May 1	Legal	Legal		$200
Arkansas	Nov 15–Apr 15	Legal	Legal		$200
Calif.	Nov 1–Apr 1	Illegal	Legal		
Colo.	Permitted	Illegal in Some Counties	Legal	MNF	
Conn.	Nov 15–Apr 1	Legal	Illegal	MNF	$200
Delaware	Oct 15–Apr 15	Legal	Legal		
DC	Oct 15–Apr 15	Legal	Illegal	MNF	
Florida	Illegal	Illegal	Legal	ML	$200
Georgia	Illegal Unless Snow or Ice	Illegal	Legal	ML	
Hawaii	Illegal	Legal	Legal		
Idaho	Oct 1–Apr 15	Legal	Legal		$200
Illinois	Illegal	Illegal	Legal		
Indiana	Oct 1–May 1	Legal	Legal		$200
Iowa	Nov 1–Apr 1	Legal	Legal		$200
Kansas	Nov 1–Apr 15	Legal	Legal	MNF	$200
Kentucky	Legal	Legal	Legal	MNF	$200
Louisiana	Illegal	Legal	Legal	ML	$200
Maine	Oct 2–Apr 30	Legal	Legal		
Maryland	Illegal Excpt W.Md. Nov 1–Mar 31	Legal	Legal	ML	$500

State	Studded Tires	Headsets	Radar Det.	Insurance	AAA Bail
Mass.	Nov 2–Apr 30	Illegal	Legal	ML	$200
Michigan	Soft Studs Nov 15–Apr 1 N. Mich. Oct 1–May 1	Legal	Legal	MNF	$200
Minn.	Illegal	Illegal	Legal	MNF	
Miss.	Illegal	Legal	Legal		
Missouri	Nov 1–Mar 31	Legal	Legal		
Montana	Oct 1–May 31	Legal	Legal	ML	$100
Nebraska	Nov 1–Mar 15	Legal	Legal		$200
Nevada	Oct 1–Apr 30	Legal	Legal	ML	
NH	Legal	Legal	Legal		
NJ	Nov 15–Apr 1	Legal	Legal	MNF	$200
NM	Legal	Legal	Legal		$200
NY	Oct 16–Apr 30	Legal	Legal	ML	
NC	Legal	Legal	Legal	ML	
ND	Oct 15–Apr 15	Legal	Legal	MNF	
Ohio	Nov 1–Apr 15	Legal	Legal		$200
Oklahoma	Nov 1–Apr 1	Legal	Legal		
Oregon	Nov 1–Apr 1	Legal	Legal		$200
Penn	Nov 1–Apr 1	Illegal	Legal	MNF	$200
RI	Nov 15–Apr 1	Illegal	Legal		
SC	Legal if Project Less Than 1/16" when compressed	Legal	Legal		
SD	Oct 15–Apr 15	Legal	Legal		
Tenn.	Oct 1–Apr 30	Legal	Legal		$200
Texas	Soft Studs Only	Legal	Legal	ML	$200
Utah	Soft Studs Oct 15–Mar 31	Legal	Legal	MNF	$200
Vermont	Legal	Legal	Legal		

State	Studded Tires	Headsets	Radar Det.	Insurance	AAA Bail
Virginia	Oct 15–Apr 15	Illegal	Illegal		$200
Wash.	Nov 1–Apr 1	Illegal	Legal		$500
Wisc.	Only Out of State Res. May Use	Legal	Legal		$200
Wyoming	Legal	Legal	Legal	ML	

Chapter Six:
Driving in Canada

Although the rules of the road in Canada are similar to those in the United States, there are important differences you should know. First, and most importantly, before driving to Canada, you should obtain from your automobile insurer an "Interprovincial Financial Responsibility Card" to show your insurance coverage. If you are involved in an accident in Canada or are stopped by the police, you will be asked to produce this as proof of insurance. Most insurance companies do not charge for providing this card.

About half the provinces in Canada require that seatbelts be fastened. Seatbelts are mandatory in British Columbia, Newfoundland, Ontario, Quebec and Saskatchewan.

Only Quebec generally prohibits right turns on red; the other provinces permit right turns on red after a stop, and with caution.

As in the United States, most Canadian jurisdictions require children to be in safety seats. The authors recommend, for safety and legal reasons, that all passengers wear seatbelts or be in safety seats.

Radar detectors are illegal in most provinces. The table below shows radar detector, studded tires and other Canadian laws:

Province	Studded Tires	Radar Detectors Legal?	Seatbelts Compulsory?	Headsets Legal?	Right Turn On Red?
Alberta	Permitted	No	No	Yes	Yes
B.C.	Oct 1–Apr 30	Yes	Yes	Yes	Yes
Manitoba	Oct 1–Apr 30	No	No	No	Yes
N.B.	Oct 16–Apr 30	Yes	No	Yes	Yes
Newfoundland	Nov 1–Apr 30	No	Yes	Yes	Yes
N.W. Territ.	Permitted	No	No	Yes	Yes
Nova Scotia	Oct 15–Apr 30	Yes	No	Yes	Yes
Ontario	Prohibited	No	Yes	Yes	Yes
Prince Edw. I.	Oct 1–May 31	No	No	Yes	Yes
Quebec	Permitted	No	Yes	No	No
Saskatchewan	Permitted	Yes	Yes	Yes	Yes
Yukon	Permitted	No	No	Yes	Yes

Chapter Seven: International Rules of the Road

The first rule of the road that you should know is whether the place you are going recognizes your driver's license, registration and license plates. The United Nations Convention on Road Traffic has simplified these rules for most countries. Many countries recognize foreign driver's licenses for a period of one year after you enter the country. In the chart below if an international driver's license is not required, you need only bring your valid driver's license, a passport and sometimes a visa. In these countries you can drive pleasure vehicles and rental cars, but not commercial vehicles.

These nations also recognize license plates and registration from other nations. When driving overseas you should apply the international distinguishing sign (oval marker) to indicate your country of origin. The following chart shows international distinguishing signs, driver's license requirements and seatbelt laws:

Country	International Distinguishing Sign	International Driver's License Required	Seatbelts Mandatory?	Drive on Left/Right?
Afghanistan	AFG	Yes	No	R
Albania	AL	No	No	R

Country	International Distinguishing Sign	International Driver's License Required	Seatbelts Mandatory?	Drive on Left/Right?
Algeria	DZ	No	No	R
Andorra	AND	No	No	R
Angola		Yes	No	R
Antigua		Yes	No	R
Argentina	RA	No	No	R
Australia	AUS	No	Yes	L
Bahamas	BS	No	No	L
Bahrain	BRN	Yes	No	R
Bangladesh	BAN	No	No	L
Barbados	BDS	Local Fee	No	L
Belgium	B	No	Yes	R
Belize		Yes	No	R
Benin	RPB	No	No	R
Bermuda	BDA	No	No	L
Bhutan	BHT	Yes	No	R
Bolivia	BOL	Yes	No	R
Botswana	RB	No	No	R
Brazil	BR	Yes*	Yes	R
British Virgin Islands	BVI	No	Yes	L
Brunei		Yes	No	R
Bulgaria	BG	Yes	No	R
Burma	BUR	Yes	No	R
Burundi	RU	Yes	No	R
Cameroun	CAM	Yes	No	R
Canada	CDN	No	In B.C., Quebec, Ont., Sask. & Newf.	R
Cape Verde		No	No	R
Caymen Islands		No	No	L

Country	International Distinguishing Sign	International Driver's License Required	Seatbelts Mandatory?	Drive on Left/Right?
Central African Republic	RCA	No	No	R
Chad	TCH	Yes	No	R
Chile	RCH	No	No	R
China	CHI	Yes	No	L
Columbia	CO	Yes	No	R
Congo	RCB	No	No	R
Costa Rica	CRG	Yes*	No	R
Cuba	C	No	No	R
Cyprus	CY	No	No	L
Czechoslovakia	CS	No	Yes	R
Denmark	DK	No	Yes	R
Djibouti		No	No	R
Dominica	WD	Yes	No	R
Dominican Republic	DOM	No	No	R
Ecuador	EC	No	No	R
Egypt	ET	No	No	R
El Salvador	ELS	Yes*	No	R
Equatorial Guinea	EDQ	Yes	No	R
Ethiopia	ETH	Yes	No	R
Fiji	FJI	No	No	L
Finland	SF	No	Yes	R
France & Territories	F	No	Yes	R
Gabon	GAB	Yes	No	R
Gambia	WAG	Yes	No	R
Germany, East (GDR)	D	Yes	No	R

Country	International Distinguishing Sign	International Driver's License Required	Seatbelts Mandatory?	Drive on Left/Right?
Germany, West (FRG)	D	No	Yes	R
Ghana	GH	No	No	R
Gibraltar	GBZ	No	Yes	L
Great Britian/ N. Ireland (U.K.)	GB	No	Yes	L
Alderney	GBA	No	Yes	L
Guernsey	GBG	No	Yes	L
Jersey	CBJ	No	Yes	L
Isle of Man	GBM	No	Yes	L
Greece	GR	No	Yes	R
Grenada	WG	No	No	L
Guatemala	GCA	No	No	R
Guinea	RG	Yes	No	R
Guinea-Bissau		No	No	R
Guyana	BRG	No	No	R
Haiti	RH	No	No	R
Honduras	HON	Yes*	No	R
Hong Kong	HK	No	Yes	L
Hungary	H	No	Yes	R
Iceland	IS	Yes	No	R
India	IND	No	No	L
Indonesia	RI	Yes	No	R
Iran	IR	Yes	No	R
Iraq	IRQ	Yes	No	R
Ireland	IRE	No	Yes	L
Israel	IL	No	Yes	R
Italy	I	No	No	R
Ivory Coast	CI	No	Yes	R

Country	International Distinguishing Sign	International Driver's License Required	Seatbelts Mandatory?	Drive on Left/Right?
Jamaica	JA	No	No	L
Japan	J	Yes	No	L
Jordan	HKJ	No	No	R
Kampuchea	K	No	No	R
Kenya	EAK	Yes	No	L
Korea	ROK	No	No	R
Kuwait	KWT	Yes	No	R
Laos	LAO	No	No	R
Lebanon	RL	No	No	R
Lesotho	LS	No	No	R
Liberia	LB	Yes	No	R
Libya	LT	Yes	No	R
Liechtenstein	FL	Yes**	No	R
Luxembourg	L	No	Yes	R
Macao		Yes	No	R
Malagasi Republic	RM	No	No	R
Malaysia	MAL	Yes	Yes	L
Malawi	MW	No	No	R
Maldive Republic	MDV	Yes	No	R
Mali	RMM	No	No	R
Mauritania	RIM	Yes	No	R
Mauritius	MS	Yes	No	L
Mexico	MEX	No	No	R
Monaco	MC	No	No	R
Mongolia	MNG	Yes	No	R
Montserrat		Yes	Yes	L
Morocco	MA	No	No	R

Country	International Distinguishing Sign	International Driver's License Required	Seatbelts Mandatory?	Drive on Left/Right?
Mozambique		No	No	L
Namibia (S.W. Africa)	SWA	No	No	R
Nepal	NEP	Yes	No	R
Netherlands	NL	No	Yes	R
Netherlands Antilles	NA	Yes	No	R
New Caledonia		No	No	R
New Zealand	NZ	No	Yes	L
Nicaragua	NIC	Yes*	No	R
Niger	NIG	No	No	R
Nigeria	WAN	Yes	No	R
Norway	N	No	Yes	R
Oman	OMN	Yes	No	R
Pakistan	PAK	Yes	No	L
Panama	PA	Yes*	No	R
Papua New Guinea		No	No	R
Paraguay	PY	No	No	R
Peru	PE	No	No	R
Philippines	PI	No	No	R
Poland	PL	No	No	R
Portugal	P	No	No	R
Qatar	Q	Yes	No	R
Romania	R	No	No	R
Rwanda	RWA	No	No	R
St. Christopher, Nevis & Anguilla		Yes	No	L
St. Lucia	WL	No	No	L

Country	International Distinguishing Sign	International Driver's License Required	Seatbelts Mandatory?	Drive on Left/Right?
St. Vincent	WV	No	No	L
San Marino	RSM	No	No	R
Sao Tome & Principe		Yes	No	R
Saudi Arabia (Men Only)	SA	Yes	No	R
Senegal	SN	No	No	R
Seychelles	SY	No	No	R
Sierra Leone	WAL	No	No	R
Singapore	SGP	No	No	L
Somalia	SP	Yes	No	R
South Africa	ZA	No	Yes	L
Spain	E	No	Yes	R
Sri Lanka	SL	No	No	R
Sudan	SUD	Yes	No	R
Swaziland (Ngwana)	SD	No	No	R
Switzerland	CH	No	Yes	R
Sweden	S	No	Yes	R
Syria	SYR	No	No	R
Taiwan	RC	No	No	R
Tanzania	EAT	Yes	No	L
Thailand	T	No	No	L
Togo	TG	No	No	L
Trinidad & Tobago	TT	No	No	L
Tunisia	TN	No	No	R
Turkey	TR	No	No	R
Uganda	EAU	No	No	L
USSR	SU	No	Yes	R

Country	International Distinguishing Sign	International Driver's License Required	Seatbelts Mandatory?	Drive on Left/Right?
United Arab Emirates	UAE	Yes	No	R
United States	USA	No	NY & PR Only	R
Upper Volta	HV	Yes	No	R
Uruguay	U	Yes*	No	R
Vatican City	V	No	No	R
Venezuela	YV	No	No	R
Vietnam	VN	No	No	R
Western Samoa	WS	Yes	No	R
Yemen Arab Republic	YMN	Yes	No	R
Yemen People's D.R.	ADN	Yes	No	R
Yugoslavia	YU	No	Yes	R
Zaire	CGO	No	No	R
Zambia	Z	Yes	No	R
Zimbabwe	ZW	No	No	R

* denotes countries which recognizes Inter-American Registration and Driver's License.

**denotes country which technically requires International Driver's License, but in reality does not.

International Driver's License

In order to drive in certain countries you will have to obtain an International Driving Permit. You can get one of these in your own country, usually through an automobile club. All that is required is the presentation of a valid driver's permit, and a small fee.

Interamerican Registration

Persons travelling on a passport from a country in the Western Hemisphere can obtain an Interamerican Registration card. This is recognized in most countries in the Western Hemisphere, and is issued only in your home country. It enables the holder to drive in other Western Hemisphere nations.

Difference Between U.S. Rules and International Rules of the Road

Although there is much in common between the American rules of the road and the International rules (Convention on Road Traffic), there are significant differences. I will only discuss the major differences in this chapter. As you can see from the road signs in chapters three and four, many of the signs are similar.

Duties at the Scene of An Accident

In the United States drivers involved in an accident are encouraged to move the vehicles out of the roadway to permit others to pass the accident scene. The international rule requires drivers to preserve evidence of fault, but also to ensure traffic safety at the scene. Until the police reach the scene of your accident (outside of the U.S.) don't move your car. Light a flare, or take other action, so that others do not compund the accident by hitting the cars.

Position on Roadway and Passing

The international rule requires motorcycles to operate on the right edge of two-lane roadways.

In the U.S. motorcycles are permitted to occupy a full lane of traffic.

The international rules severely limit lane changes. Under these rules a driver, not in the right-hand lane (left hand lane in those countries who drive on the left), can change lanes only to turn or to park. In the United States drivers can change lanes when it can be done safely, and generally can pass on the right. Outside the U.S. you are not generally permitted to pass on the right, except when traffic is congested, or where a vehicle is turning left.

Right of Way

The law everywhere (except countries where they drive on left) requires drivers turning left to yield to oncoming vehicles. The international rule also requires right-turners to yield: if a left-turner and a right-turner are entering the same lane, both must yield.

Stopping

The international rules prohibits abrupt stops which are not necessary for safety reasons. They also require a driver who intends to slow down to first make certain that he can do so safely. In the United States the driver of the following vehicle has the duty to follow at a safe distance, even if the other vehicle stops suddenly for no apparent reason. This explains why Americans are shocked by how closely they are followed on highways outside of the United States.

Lighting

The international rule permits the use of "position" lights (parking lights in the United States), instead of headlights at night, when the roadway is properly lighted. This explains why European drivers often turn their headlights off in cities. The international rule does permit use of headlights in cities, but Americans using this headlights will often be flashed at in foreign cities.

In Sweden and Finland, however, you are required to use your headlights even in broad daylight. This is recommended, but not required, in Denmark and Norway.

Chapter Eight: What You Must do After an Accident in the United States

by Edward F. Kearney, former Executive Director
National Committee on Uniform Traffic Laws
and Ordinances

In a recent year in the United States, there were an estimated 16,400,000 accidents involving 28,300,000 drivers. Because there were 114,000,000 licensed drivers, one driver in four may have been involved in a crash that year. Thus, the likelihood of your being involved in a crash during the next four or five years is very high.

Accidents are sudden events. A minor one is traumatic, even for an experienced driver. If someone has been injured, there is additional emotional involvement.

For these reasons, every driver should fully understand and memorize his or her primary responsibilities. Every driver involved in an accident must:

1. Stop,
2. Identify himself, and
3. Aid any injured person.

Failure to perform these duties at the scene of an accident carries severe legal penalties. If a person has been hurt, the penalty under the *Uniform*

Vehicle Code is $100 to $5,000 and/or 30 days to one year in jail. (The *Uniform Vehicle Code* (UVC) is model legislation for the United States. Nearly every state has adopted most provisions of the UVC.) Most states require a convicted person's license to be revoked.

Under certain circumstances, a driver involved in a crash must also notify the police as soon as possible and within five or ten days, file a written accident report. In addition to these legal requirements, your insurance company may specify additional requirements for notice of accidents.

The Duty to Stop

Every driver of a vehicle involved in an accident resulting in death, injury or any damage to property must stop immediately.

The stop must be made as close to the scene as possible. In all accidents, involved vehicles must not obstruct traffic any more than necessary. If possible, do not leave your car in a lane used by moving traffic. Park on a shoulder. Pull clear of an intersection. It is not only unlawful for movable vehicles to be left in the roadway, it is also inconsiderate and dangerous. Though it is not necessary to leave vehicles where they were at the point of impact until a police officer arrives, their location should be noted for subsequent reference in preparing accident reports. If your car can't be moved, arrange to have it towed from the scene.

The law requires involved drivers to remain at the scene of the accident until they have identified themselves and aided any injured persons.

The Duty to Identify Yourself

A driver involved in an accident must give his or her name, address and the registration number of the vehicle he is driving to any person injured in the accident or to the driver, occupant or person attending any vehicle or property damaged in the crash.

If any person is dead, unconscious or otherwise not able to receive the information, the driver must call the police and give them the same information.

If your driver's license is available and is requested, it must be shown. If there is a police officer at the scene or investigating the accident, the information and your license must be given to the officer.

If unattended property has been damaged, you must either locate the owner (and provide the information identifying you and your vehicle) or you must attach a written note to the damaged property and immediately notify the police. The note should contain your name, address and vehicle registration number.

It is recommended that a driver never leave the scene of an accident without identifying himself or herself. Even if you leave to call an ambulance or the police, you should leave something at the scene that will identify you to avoid any possible misunderstanding about your intentions.

The Duty to Aid
Any Injured Person

Every driver of a vehicle involved in an accident must render reasonable assistance to any person injured in the accident if it is apparent the person needs treatment or if the person requests it. This assistance must be rendered by making arrangements for transporting the person to a hospital or doctor or, if necessary, by transporting the injured person there yourself. In most instances, you should simply call for an ambulance. However, in some cases, it may be preferable for you to transport the injured person to a hospital or physician if you can, particularly if the injuries are minor or if you are a great distance from a telephone. As a general rule, you should not attempt to move a person who is unconscious or seriously hurt. See the pink pages of this book for first aid procedures.

The duty of a driver to stop and aid injured persons is one of the first motor vehicle laws adopted by the states. The breach of this duty is inhumane and borders on being immoral. Prompt medical attention can mean the difference between life and death to a significant number of persons hurt in auto crashes.

Immediate Notice to The Police

If any person has been injured or killed in an accident, an involved drive must notify the nearest police station by using the quickest means of communication, usually by telephone or citizen's band radio. This duty should be performed immediately after identifying yourself and aiding the injured. Most people call the police to summon an ambulance, thereby complying with two duties at the same time. Many areas of the United States have adopted the 911 emergency number. Dial 911. If that doesn't work, try calling the operator.

Though some states do not require immediate notice to the police of accidents resulting only in damage to property, a majority require such notice when damage equals or exceeds a specified dollar amount which usually is $100 or $200.

As previously noted, a driver involved in an accident must also notify the police after unattended property has been damaged when its owner cannot be located. If you damage a traffic-control device (such as a stop sign or signal) or highway appurtenance (such as a guardrail), you should attach a note to it and notify the police so it can be repaired. The failure of drivers to provide this notice is illegal and can cause other drivers to crash and be injured.

Duty to File Written Accident Report

Every driver of a vehicle involved in certain accidents must file a written accident report with the appropriate agency in the state where the accident occurred. The report must use an official form and must contain all information requested in the form. Copies of the form can usually be obtained from the state department of motor vehicles or a local police station. Often an officer will bring these forms to the scene of the accident.

The requirements for a written report applies to drivers involved in an accident resulting in death, injury or damage to property of $100 or more. A few states require written reports of accidents causing any damage to property.

This written report generally must be mailed to a state agency within five or ten days after the accident. To help you fill out the government form, and for insurance and legal reasons, two accident forms are included here.

Because you may not gather all the above information at the scene from other drives occupants, you should at least get their addresses and telephone numbers so it can subsequently be secured when filling out the form. If any of the witnesses were bystanders or non-involved vehicles, be sure to get their names, addresses and telephone numbers at the scene of the accident or there will be no way to contact them later.

Written reports from drivers are used by the state primarily for accident prevention purposes. They are confidential and not open to public inspection. Contents of the report also may not be used as evidence in court except to prosecute a person for making a false report.

Giving false information in a written report is illegal. A person who fails to file a written report is guilty of a misdemeanor and his driver's license may be suspended until the report is filed.

Municipalities in some states may require a written accident report or a copy of the report sent to the state. Make several photocopies of the accident report before mailing it to the state.

"Involved in an Accident"

The duties described in this Chapter apply to drivers of vehicles "involved in an accident." What does that mean?

If you are behind the wheel of a vehicle that comes into physical contact with another vehicle, pedestrian or object, you are involved in an accident. If you are driving and cause or contribute to a crash by another driver, you are involved in an accident even though there is no physical contact involving your car. For instance, if you are double parked, a car drives on the left side of the street to avoid it, and collides with an oncoming car, you are involved in an accident. Similarly, if you pass a car and force it off the road into a pole, you are involved in an accident. Being "involved in an accident" has nothing to do with causing it.

In most states, the duties described in this Chapter apply to accidents occurring everywhere in the state, on the highways and off, including shopping centers, driveways and parking lots.

Notifying Your Insurance Company

The company insuring the vehicle you are driving also must be notified of the accident. Insurance is provided by means of a contract and it usually requires the person insured to notify the company of an accident. This notice enables the insurer to verify coverage, investigate the accident, and make arrangements to pay claims.

If an accident causes death or personal injury, most insurance companies require oral notice by telephone to a local office or special number that will be provided to you in advance. This call should be made as soon as reasonably possible after stopping at the scene, identifying yourself, rendering aid to the injured and notifying the police. During this call, you will be asked to provide much of the same information previously mentioned and an indication where injured persons have been taken for treatment.

If an accident causes only property damage, you should notify your insurance company by telephone, within a reasonable time. Unless there is extensive property damage, it will be all right to call during business hours. However, you may want to call sooner if your car has been rendered inoperable or if you need assistance.

An unreasonably long delay in notifying your insurance company can have adverse consequences.

Your insurance company will want a written accident report. Though some insurers will accept a copy of the written report filed with the state, others want a report on their own form.

Accident Procedure*

Use the accident information form (at the end of this chapter) to record the names, addresses, telephone numbers and other information for the other drivers, injured persons and witnesses. Make sure that you report the accident to the police and to your insurance company. If the accident is minor, and you are certain that you were at fault and caused the accident, and you fear that your insurance premiums will increase, you can pay for the damage without notifying your insurance company. However, if it turns out that the "uninjured" victims files a claim against you, you may not be covered by your insurance company because you notified them too late. Be aware of the risks involved in failing to notify your insurance company.

---

*This section was added by the editors.

DO NOT reveal the extent of your insurance coverage, unless required to do so by the police at the scene of the accident.

DO NOT ADMIT responsibility, or apologize to anyone about the accident. Make no statements to anyone but the police and your own insurance company or attorney.

WHEN TALKING TO THE POLICE be very careful what you say. It is generally better to say nothing than to make false statements to a police officer. You must identify yourself, and show your driver's license. In some states you must produce proof of financial responsibility, or of insurance coverage. Otherwise you do not have to say anything. If you feel that the poice are accusing you of a serious crime, or if someone has been badly hurt, ask to talk to your lawyer **before** making a statement to the police. Anything you say can, **and will** be used against you either in a criminal case or in a civil case.

CONCLUSION

A driver's principal duties at the scene of a crash are to stop, identify himself and render aid to injured persons. Under certain circumstances, you must notify the police and you also should contact the company insuring the car you were driving.

Involvement in a crash will delay your trip. Even a minor crash can result in preparing two written reports, one for your insurance company and one for the state. Avoid this senseless waste of time by following all rules of the road and by being prepared for other persons to violate them. An accident is a hassle.

Accident Information Form

DATE OF ACCIDENT: _____ TIME _____ AM

WHICH POLICE DEPARTMENT MADE ACCIDENT REPORT?

NAME OF POLICE OFFICERS PRESENT: BADGE NUMBERS

WHERE DID ACCIDENT OCCUR?

STREET(S)_____CITY_____STATE:_____

OTHER VEHICLES:

VEHICLE NUMBER 1:

DRIVER OF OTHER   HOME
VEHICLE:_____   TELEPHONE:_____

                              WORK
ADDRESS:_____   TELEPHONE:_____

EMPLOYER:_____DRIVER'S LICENSE:_____

                              STATE:_____

LICENSE PLATE:_____   STATE:_____

OWNER OF VEHICLE:_____ADDRESS:_____

_____

DESCRIBE DAMAGE:_____

_____

VEHICLE NUMBER 2:

DRIVER OF OTHER
VEHICLE:_____

HOME
TELEPHONE:_____

ADDRESS:_____

WORK
TELEPHONE:_____

EMPLOYER:_____DRIVER'S LICENSE:_____

STATE:_____

LICENSE PLATE:_____   STATE:_____

OWNER OF VEHICLE:_____ADDRESS:_____

_____

DESCRIBE DAMAGE:_____

_____

VEHICLE NUMBER 3:

DRIVER OF OTHER
VEHICLE:_____

HOME
TELEPHONE:_____

ADDRESS:_____

WORK
TELEPHONE:_____

EMPLOYER:_____DRIVER'S LICENSE:_____

STATE:_____

LICENSE PLATE:_____   STATE:_____

OWNER OF VEHICLE:_____ADDRESS:_____

_____

DESCRIBE DAMAGE:_____

_____

PERSONS INJURED:

1. NAME:_____TELEPHONE:_____

ADDRESS:_____CITY:_____STATE:_____

2. NAME:_____TELEPHONE:_____

ADDRESS:_____CITY:_____STATE:_____

3. NAME:_____TELEPHONE:_____

ADDRESS:_____CITY:_____STATE:_____

OCCUPANTS OF ALL VEHICLES:_____

1. NAME:_____TELEPHONE:_____

ADDRESS:_____CITY:_____STATE:_____

2. NAME:_____TELEPHONE:_____

ADDRESS:_____CITY:_____STATE:_____

3. NAME:_____TELEPHONE:_____

ADDRESS:_____CITY:_____STATE:_____

4. NAME_____TELEPHONE:_____

ADDRESS:_____CITY:_____STATE:_____

OTHER WITNESSES:_____

1. NAME:_____TELEPHONE:_____

ADDRESS:_____CITY:_____STATE:_____

2. NAME:_____TELEPHONE:_____

ADDRESS:_____CITY:_____STATE:_____

3. NAME:_____TELEPHONE:_____

ADDRESS:_____CITY:_____STATE:_____

4. NAME:_____TELEPHONE:_____

ADDRESS:_____CITY:_____STATE:_____

Chapter Nine:
What You Should Do After An Accident Outside the U.S.

Unlike accidents in the U.S., the international rules requires drivers to preserve evidence of fault by keeping the cars in the positions they were after impact. Until the police reach the scene of your accident, don't move your car. You also have a duty to ensure that other vehicles don't compound the accident. Light a flare, flag cars away from the scene, or take other action, so that others do not compound the accident by hitting the cars again.

If the accident involves only property damage you do not have a duty to notify the police. You do, however, have the duty to stop, and to identify yourself, if asked. If there is injury or death you have a duty to notify the police. In most countries, if there are only minor injuries, those involved in the accident can mutually agree not to notify the police.

Use the accident information form (at the end of chapter eight) to record the names, addresses, telephone numbers and other information for the other drivers, injured persons and witnesses. Make sure that you report the accident to the police and to your insurance company. If the accident is minor, and you are certain that you were at fault and caused the accident, and you fear that your insurance premiums will increase, you can pay for the damage without notifying your insurance company. However, if it turns out that the "uninjured" victim files a claim against you, you may not be covered by your insurance company because you notified them too late. Be aware of the risks involved in failing to notify your insurance company.

DO NOT reveal the extent of your insurance coverage, unless required to do so by the police at the scene of the accident.

DO NOT ADMIT responsibility, or apologize to anyone about the accident. Make no statements to anyone but the police and your own insurance company or attorney.

WHEN TALKING TO THE POLICE be very careful what you say. It is generally better to say nothing than to make false statements to a police officer. You must identify yourself, and show your driver's license. In some states you must produce proof of financial responsibility, or of insurance coverage. Otherwise you do not have to say anything. If you feel that the police are accusing you of a serious crime, or if someone has been badly hurt, ask to talk to your lawyer **before** making a statement to the police. Anything you say can, **and will** be used against you either in a criminal case or in a civil case.

Outside of the United States you do not have to report accidents that occurred on private property. You have no duty to exhibit your driver's license. If no one was injured you do not have to stay at the scene of the accident. If only unattended property is damaged, you do not have to notify the police. If there are only minor personal injuries, and no one wants the police notified, you do not have a duty to call the police.

Chapter Ten:
What You Should Do When Stopped by the Police

Getting stopped by the police is rarely an enjoyable occasion. When you see that the police are behind you and signaling you to pull over, your heart starts beating faster. Try to be calm and polite. You may feel like screaming and arguing, but try to resist the impulse. Be polite. Smile. Excuses may be appropriate, but don't give ridiculous ones.

Also, before you turn off your engine and leave your car **make certain it is really the police** who have stopped you. Ask to see a picture identification card, not just a badge. Anyone can buy an official-looking badge; too many sharp operators impersonate the police to stop and prey on motorists.

If you are in a foreign country, and are not fluent in the language, try to express that fact. You should have a phrase book with you whenever you are in a country where you do not speak the language. If the charge may be serious ask for an interpreter [interprete, por favor (in Spanish); interprete, s'il vous plait (in French); Dolmetcher, bitte (German)]. You can also ask to see a lawyer.

Speeding

Speeding is one of the most common traffic offenses. Police officers have heard every speeding excuse in the book: some they laugh at, and others make them change their minds. The good excuses are:

■ You are taking a pregnant woman to a hospital;

■ You are taking an injured/sick person to a hospital;

■ You have a court emergency;

■ You are on emergency government business; and

■ Your speedometer is broken.

If you have a medical emergency most police officers will not detain you. Many will offer to escort you to the nearest hospital. If you have been summoned to court, or are on official court business, show court papers to the officer. If you are on legislative business, you may be immune from arrest. Show the police your official identification and explain the nature of the emergency. In many places government employees will not be detained or arrested if on official business. Always show your identification card, be polite and explain your emergency.

Mechanical excuses, such as "my speedometer is not working" will work on occasion. Be prepared to take the officer for a test ride to confirm the mechanical problem.

Alcohol Offenses

Driving under the influence of alcohol or drugs, and driving while intoxicated, are serious offenses. **Refusing to take a breath or other alcohol test is often cause for immediate arrest.** Even if you are not intoxicated it is a separate traffic offense to refuse to take a test. Refusing the test will also reduce your legal rights. If you are tested improperly you can challenge the accuracy of the test in court. However, if you refuse to take a test, you often automatically will lose your driving privileges.

Do not say anything to the police that can be used against you. You only are required to show your identification to the police and submit to an alcohol or drug test. You have the right to call your lawyer and your spouse or a friend.

Searches

The law of automobile searches varies from jurisdiction to jurisdiction. Further, it changes, often. The U.S. law of automobile searches is so complicated that searching a hatchback vehicle without a warrant may be legal and searching another type of car would require a warrant.

If you are in a hurry and have nothing to hide, let the police search your car. If you have something that you do not want the police to see, **do not consent to a search of your vehicle.** Don't fight with the police. Politely ask if they have a search warrant. If they insist on searching without obtaining a warrant, make sure that they know that you do not consent, but don't try to stop them. You can later challenge the legality of the search. Resisting the police, even if they are acting illegally, is often a criminal offense. Only resist in self-defense, when you feel that you will be seriously injured if you don't.

Chapter Eleven:
Automobile Warranties

Next to your home, a car is usually your largest investment. With economy cars selling for $10,000, it is indeed frustrating when the damn vehicle doesn't work properly. There are eleven different steps that you can take when you new, or fairly new, automobile seems to be in the repair shop more often than it is in your garage. These steps can be pursued, not necessarily in this order:

1. Complain to the dealer

2. Complain the manufacturer's zone or regional representatives

3. Complain to the main headquarters of the manufacturer

4. Return your lemon

5. If in the United States, file a complaint with the Automotive Consumer Action Program (AUTOCAP)

6. Write to the U.S. Federal Trade Commission

7. Refuse to pay your car loan (in certain cases)

8. Write to the U.S. National Highway Traffic Safety Administration

9. Write to the U.S. Environmental Protection Agency

10. File a complaint with a Consumer Protection Office

11. File Suit

The Dealer

First, unless your car is a total disaster, you should give your dealer an opportunity to repair the car. If the needed repair work is covered by the manufacturer's warranty, the dealer should make the repair. Even if the warranty period has expired, the dealer may be able to make the repair under a so-called "secret" warranty. A secret warranty is made when a manufacturer has had repeated problems with a particular component of the car. It is secret because dealers are told to charge for the repairs unless the customer complains. So by all means, make a vocal complaint. If you suspect that other people are experiencing the same problem you can call or write the Automobile Owners Action Council, or the Center for Auto Safety. Their addresses are:

Automobile Owners Action Council
1010 Vermont Avenue, N.W.
Washington, DC 20005
(202) 638-5550

Center for Auto Safety
1223 DuPont Circle Building
Washington, DC 20036
(202) 659-1126

You can also write to the Better Business Bureau, or to an action line. Send copies of your complaint letter to as many of these organizations as you want; it might strike a nerve somewhere and provoke assistance.

While the dealer who sold you the car should be responsive to your complaints you can go to any dealer who sells the car that you own. A large dealer may have had more experience with your type of problem. Some dealers have better service departments than others; if you are unhappy with one dealer, try another.

Manufacturer's Representatives

Every auto manufacturer has an internal system for handling consumer complaints. Auto dealers are supervised by regional or zone representatives of the manufacturers. Your dealer will give you the name of the zone rep who services it. The zone rep may be able to handle your complaint by phone, or he may want to meet you at a dealership to inspect your car. A zone or regional representative has the power to authorize warranty repairs, even when your car is not in the warranty period.

Corporate Headquarters

Occasionally, writing to the president of an auto manufacturer gets results. But the standard route is to write to the customer relations office at the corporation's headquarters. A sample complaint letter is included at the end of this chapter.

Returning Your Lemon

If your problems are substantial, and you have been deprived of the use of your car for a long time, you may be able to take back your lemon for a refund or exchange. Before returning your car, you should consult with an attorney. Returning a car is risky because you may still be liable for car payments while the dispute is being worked out. Taking your car back is a last resort which should only be attempted when it seems that your problems are insoluble. If you car in turned in make sure that you offer the dealer the keys and title, remove your license plates, and notify your lender and insurance company.

Autocaps

There are 32 regional automobile consumer action programs, or Autocaps, across the United States. Each Autocap has a panel composed of half industry representatives and half consumer representatives, which will review your complaint. These panels make a decision within three or four weeks which is usually followed by the manufacturer or dealer, but its decision is not binding on you. If you disagree with the decision of the Autocap panel, you can pursue other remedies, through agencies or in court.

The U.S. Federal
Trade Commission

The U.S. Federal Trade Commission (FTC) will investigate cases where warranties are not lived up to or where there have been false or misleading advertisements. The FTC will not usually resolve an individual complaint, but it will step in where a pattern of fraud or warranty violations develops. The FTC has regional offices in major cities and a national office in Washington. The national office has a warranty project. If you have a warranty problem write to:

Warranty Project
Bureau of Consumer Protection
Federal Trade Commission
Washington, DC 20580

Concerning false advertising or other fradulent practices, write to a regional FTC office.

When You Have a Right to Refuse to Pay Your Car Loan

If you bought your car in the United States, and the car dealer arranges your loan, you legally are entitled to stop making car payments when there are serious problems with the car. You have a right to stop making payments on your GM car when GMAC provided financing, your Ford product when Ford Motor Credit made your loan, or when Chrysler Credit lent money for your Chrysler product. However, if your credit union or bank made the car loan directly to you, you must continue to make car payments, even when your car is a lemon through and through.

The U.S. National Highway Traffic Safety Administration

The Environment Protection Agency can help you resolve auto complaints that, at first glance, do not appear to concern the environment. For example, if your car with 40,000 miles on it, needs a valve job because it is burning oil, the EPA may be able to get the work done at no cost to you, even though your warranty has expired. The Clean Air laws require all cars to meet emission requirements for 5 or 50,000 miles. A car that burns oil in excess probably cannot meet the emission limits. Even if you bought the car used, the EPA can still help. If you car is smoking excessively or burning too much oil, or your catalytic converter does not work anymore, write the

EPA a letter. To confirm that your car fails to comply with the air quality laws, you should get it inspected at your state's inspection service (if your state has an inspection program) or at a private inspection service. The address to send your complaint to is:

Director
Mobile Source Enforcement
Environmental Protection Agency
Washington, DC 20460

Consumer Protection Agencies

Every state in the United States has offices to handle consumers complaints. If you have failed elsewhere, your state or local office may be able to help you. A massive case against General Motors began in Illinois when a consumer complained that his Oldsmobile had a Chevy engine in it. The Attorney General of Illinois filed a class action suit against GM, which was settled quickly. Each Oldsmobile owner who received a Chevy engine also received a check from General Motors to compensate for the switch. GM now informs consumers that the engine in its cars may have been manufactured by other GM divisions, and that your Cadillac may have a Buick engine. It only takes one irate consumer to make a difference.

Taking Legal Action

If all else has failed, you should bring all your repair records and other documents to a lawyer. A half-hour consultation should be worthwhile.

The lawyer may convince you that do not have a case, or may think the case is so good that he or she will represent you on a contingency fee basis. A contingency fee means the lawyer only gets paid if there is a victory. If there is a warranty related problem, the U.S. Magnuson-Moss Warranty Act provides that if you win the case the auto company must pay for the lawyer's fees, court costs, and damages. The Automobile Owners Action Council, the Center for Auto Safety, or your local Bar Association may be able to supply you with the names of a few lawyers who will be able to represent you. If there is a small amount at stake, less than $1000, you may want to file a small claim against the dealer and the manufacturer.

Roadside Hazards

Occasionally your car is damaged by an obstruction on the highway, or by the highway itself. Potholes, trolley tracks, and other danagerous road conditions may cause auto accidents or otherwise damage your car. I have brought successful lawsuits against cities for the unsafe conditions of their roads. However, in some states, cities are immune from suit. If your car has been damaged because of unsafe roadways, discuss your rights and remedies with a lawyer in your area.

Letter to Auto Manufacturer

Name_____
Address_____
Date:_____

Consumer Affairs Office
Automobile Manufacturer

RE: Vehicle Identification Number_____
    Model, year_____
    _____

Dear_____,

    I purchased the above-described automobile on_____and have brought it back to the dealer _____ times to correct _____.
    I have lost_____days from work in order to have the car repaired. My salary is_____per day; I have therefore lost $_____in time lost from work. In addition I have had to rent a car for $_____per days for_____days, or a total of $_____.
    Enclosed are copies of repair bills, work orders and_____which confirm these problems.
    I want you to either replace the car with a new one, refund my purchase price of $_____, or pay me $_____for the damages that I have suffered. I expect your reply by _____ _____. If I do not have a

satisfactory response from you by then, I will proceed to seek relief from a court or agency with
jurisdiction over the matter.

Sincerely yours,

(Signature)
NAME
cc: Automobile Owners Action Council
    Center for Auto Safety
    Action Line

Chapter Twelve: Selling or Buying a Car

Are you selling your car? I get many calls from clients who want to sell a vehicle, asking if they should have a contract. The answer is always an emphatic "yes," since problems can often arise in any sale entered into without a written agreement. For example, one client sold a used car, and about two days later, the car developed many mechanical problems. The client was sued by the buyer for knowingly selling a defective car and for breach of warranty. After several conferences the case was settled by refunding $200 of the purchase price to the buyer, and the client was charged $300 in legal fees. This case easily could have been avoided.

Whenever you are selling a used car your should have a written contract.

Contract for Sale of a Vehicle

If you are the seller, you should limit your liability by selling the personal property *"as is,"* which means that you are making no representations as to the condition of the property. Once the seller conveys the property sold in *"as is"* condition and receives payment, he is generally not liable for anything that happens to the property after it has been delivered to the buyer.

A contract for sale of a vehicle is recommended when you sell your car or truck. A form contract is included in the chapter. This agreement does not include a mechanical warranty, so the car is sold "as is"—what you see is what you get—with no warranties being expressed concerning mechanical condition of the vehicle.

This form is designed to eliminate the problems discussed previously. The provision entitled "Warranty of Title" means that the seller of the vehicle owns the property outright that he is selling. You cannot sell something you do not own; this particular paragraph simply states that you own the property and will defend your ownership against anyone else who might come along and claim ownership.

Once this contract is signed by both parties and the property is exchanged, the seller is no longer responsible for the condition or repair of the property.

Buyer Beware!

Before buying a used car, check it out thoroughly. Either take a mechanic with you to inspect the vehicle or take the car to the mechanic before signing a contract to buy it. If the seller won't let you have a mechanic inspect the car, don't buy it unless the price is low enough to make it a good purchase even if it needs a new engine and transmission.

If you buy a used car from a used car dealer, you may get a thirty- or ninety-day warranty. You will probably pay more for a used car from a dealer than from an individual, so shop around. Don't buy the first car that you see.

Ask questions. Is the owner the original owner? Does the owner have a complete service record for the vehicle? Is the odometer mileage accurate? Does the car use much oil? How much? Was the car ever in an accident? If the owner lies to you in answering these questions, you may be able to sue him for fraud.

Seller Beware!

Tell the truth about your car. Show the potential buyer the service records. If you intentionally mislead the buyer about the car, or set the odometer back, the buyer can sue you for fraud. You are not required to volunteer every negative fact or thought about the car, but if you are asked, you must supply accurate information.

Bill of Sale

A bill of sale is often needed by a department of motor vehicles in the state, province or county where the buyer wants the vehicle to be licensed. A form bill of sale is included in this chapter which meets the requirements of motor vehicle departments for licensing. This is useful for two purposes. First, it limits the liability of the seller; the seller is merely saying, "I own the automobile and no one else has a claim of ownership." Second, this bill of sale, showing the purchase price, may be presented by the buyer to a department of motor vehicles for sales tax and ownership purposes. This bill of sale says nothing about the condition of the vehicle for the reasons discussed above. The bill of sale is also useful as a receipt.

We suggest that you use contract for sale and a bill of sale together, if you are selling or buying a vehicle. This will define your liability, as well as provide a receipt for proof of purchase. The receipt comes in especially handy regarding taxes—if you do not have a receipt, some states will decide for themselves how much the vehicle is worth. If you happened to make a good deal on the vehicle and did not have a bill of sale or receipt, you would end up paying more tax than you should, simply because you had no proof of how much money you actually paid.

Transferring Title

Most titles to automobiles have an assignment form on the back. An assignment of the title is required for a new title to be issued.

When you buy or sell a vehicle you should be sure that the title, as well as the vehicle, is properly transferred. While laws vary, the title must generally include the selling price, the name of the purchaser, and the name of the seller, and it must be witnessed by a notary public.

CONTRACT FOR SALE OF VEHICLE (NO MECHANICAL WARRANTY)

1. **Buyer and Seller**_____(seller) sells and delivers the vehicle described in Paragraph 2 to _____ (buyer).

2. **Description of Vehicle.** The vehicle being sold and delivered by this contract is described as follows:

Make:_____

Serial Number:_____

Body Type:_____

Year Manufactured:_____

3. **Price.**_____ (buyer) agrees to pay _____ (seller) the sum of $_____ for the vehicle described in Paragraph 2.

4. **Warranty of Title.** Seller warrants that he (she) is the legal owner of this vehicle, that the vehicle is free from all claims, that he (she) has the right to sell this vehicle and he (she) warrants and will defend the title, in court if necessary, against claims of any person.

5. **Mechanical Warranty.** The vehicle is sold in "as is" condition. The seller makes no warranties as to the condition of this vehicle.

_____ DATE
SELLER

_____ DATE
BUYER

BILL OF SALE FOR VEHICLE

In exchange for $_____, receipt of which is acknowledged by this Bill of Sale,

_____ (seller) sells and delivers to

_____ (buyer) the following vehicle:

Make:_____

Serial Number:_____

Body Type:_____

Year Manufactured:_____

Seller warrants that he (she) is the legal owner of this vehicle, that the vehicle is free from all claims, that he (she) has the right to sell this vehicle, and he (she) warrants and will defend the title, in court if necessary, against claims of any person.

_____
DATE

_____
SELLER

Chapter Thirteen: Automobile Associations Throughout the World

If you are a member of an automobile association, like the American Automobile Association (AAA), many foreign auto association will provide you with services. Some of these auto associations will charge you a fee for certain services, while others will give you complimentary maps and road service. Make sure that you bring your automobile association card with you when driving out of the country. The below chart lists automobile associations by country, but does not list every auto club. Some auto associations not listed below will still provide you with service. I have attempted to list at least one organization in each country.

Country	Name of Association	City	Telephone
Algeria	Touring Club D'Algerie	Algiers	64-08-37
Andorra	Automobile Club D'Andorra	La Vella	20-890
Argentina	Automovile Club Argentino	Buenos Aires	821-6061
Australia	*Australian Automobile Assn.	Sydney	(02)290-0123
		Melbourne	(03)607-2211
		Adelaide	(08)223-4555
		Brisbane	(07)221-1511
		Perth	(09)325-0551

Country	Name of Association	City	Telephone
Austria	*Osterreicher Automil-Motorrad-und Touring Club (OAMTC)	Vienna Salzburg Innsbruck	(0222)95-40 (06222)20-5-01 (05222)44-5-21
Bahamas	Bahamas Automobile Club	Nassau	325-0514
Bangladesh	Automobile Assoc. of Bengladesh	Dacca	243482
Barbados	Barbados Automobile Assoc.	Bridgetown	6-46-40
Belgium	Royal Automobile Club de Belgique	Brussels	02/230.08.10
Bolivia	Automovil Club Boliviano	La Paz	351-667
Brazil	Automovel Club do Brasil	Rio de Janeiro	297-4455
Bulgaria	Union of Bulgarian Automobilists	Sofia	87.88.01
Canada	*Canadian Automobile Assoc.	Nationwide:	(800) 336-4357
Chile	Automovil Club de Chile	Santiago	749516
Columbia	Automovil Club de Colombia	Bogota	232-6773
Costa Rica	Automovil-Touring Club de Costa Rica	San Jose	3570
Cuba	Automovil y Aero Club de Cuba	Havana	61-2551
Cyprus	Cyprus Automobile Assoc.	Nicosia	021-52-521
Czechoslovakia	Ustredni Automotoklub CSSR	Prague	223544-7
Denmark	*Forenede Danske Motorejere (FDM)	Copenhagen	(01)38-21-12
Eduador	Automovil Club de Ecuador	Quito	527-408
Egypt	Automobile et Touring Club of Egypt	Cairo	743176
El Salvador	Automovile Club de el Salvador	San Salvador	23-8077
Ethiopia	Automobile-Club Eritreo	Asmarra	11615
Finland	Autolitto, Auto & Touring Club of Finland	Helsinki	694-0022
France	Automobile Club de France	Paris	265-34-70
Germany (West)	Allgemeiner-Deutscher	Munich	089-76-76-76

Country	Name of Association	City	Telephone
(FRG)	Automobil-Club (ADAC)	Berlin	030-86-86-86
		Frankfurt	0611-74-30-1
		Hamburg	040-23-9-99
		Stuttgart	0711-28-00-11
Ghana	Automobile Assn of Ghana	Accra	75983
Great Britain (U.K.)	*Automobile Assoc. (AA)	London	01-891-1400
		Wales	BR-297272
		Scotland	041-812-0101
Greece	Auto & Touring Club of Greece (ELPA)	Athens	01-7791615
Guatemala	Club de Automovilisimo	Guatemala	83373
Hong Kong	Hong-Kong Auto Assoc.	Hong Kong	5-743394
Hungary	Magyar Autoklub	Budapest	152-040
Iceland	Iceland Automobile Assoc.	Reykjavik	91-299999
India	Auto Association of India	Calcutta	47-9012
		New Delhi	42063
		Bombay	29-1085
		Madras	293899
Indonesia	Ikatan Motor Indonesia	Jakarta	58-11-02
Iran	Touring & Auto Club of Iran	Teheran	679-142
Iraq	Iraq Auto & Touring Assoc.	Bagdad	35862
Ireland	*Automobile Association	Dublin	779481
Israel	*Auto & Touring Club of Israel (MEMSI)	Tel-Aviv	(03)622961
		Jerusalem	(02)222421
		Haifa	(04)523224
Italy	*Auto Club D'Italia (ACI)	Rome	(06)5110510
		Florence	(055)672813
		Milan	(02)793966
		Turin	(011)546385
		Venice	(041)708828
		Bologna	(051)387651
		Genova	(010)566707
Japan	*Japanese Auto Federation (JAF)	Tokyo	03-436-2811
Jordan	Royal Auto Club of Jordan	Amman	815410
Kenya	Automobile Assoc. of Kenya	Nairobi	742926

Country	Name of Association	City	Telephone
Korea (South)	Korea Auto Assoc.	Seoul	965-7219
Kuwait	Kuwait Int'l Touring & Auto Club	Kuwait	832-406
Lebanon	Auto & Touring Club of Lebanon	Beirut	221-698
Libya	Auto & Touring Club of Libya	Tripoli	33310
Liechtenstein	Automobil-Club Furstentums Liechtenstein	Vaduz	(075)2-60-66
Luxembourg	*Automobile Club du Grande Duche de Luxembourg (ACL)	Bertrange	
Madagascar	Auto Club of Madagascar	Antananarivo	420-30
Malaysia	Auto Assoc. of Malaysia	Kuala Lumpur	781055
Malta	Malta Auto. Federation	St. Pauls Bay	
Mauritius	Auto Assoc. of Mauritius	Port Louis	2-4173
Mexico	Asociacion Nacional Auto-Movilistica	Mexico City	546-99-65
Monaco	Automobile-Club de Monaco	Monaco	30-32-20
Morocco	Royal Moroccan Auto Club	Casablanca	25.00.30
Nepal	Auto Assoc. of Nepal	Katmandu	11093
Netherlands	*Koninklijke Nederlandse Toeristenbond (ANWB)	The Hague Amsterdam	(070)26-44-26 (020)17-31-35
New Zealand	*New Zealand Auto Assoc.	Aukland Wellington Christchurch	(09)796-107 (04)847-726 (03)791-280
Norway	*Norges Automobil-Forbund (NAF)	Oslo Bergen Stavanger	(02)33-70-80 (05)23-36-55 (045)20-108
Pakistan	Auto Assoc. of Pakistan Karachi Auto Assoc.	Lahore Karachi	414854 23-21-73
Panama	Assoc. Sportive Automobile Panameenne	Panama	27-24-83
Paraguay	Touring & Automovile Club Paraguayo	Asuncion	26-075
Peru	Touring & Automovile Club del Peru	Lima	40-3270

Country	Name of Association	City	Telephone
Philippines	Philippine Motor Assoc.	Manila	60-97-02
Poland	Polski Zwiazek Motorwy	Warsaw	49-93-61
Portugal	Automovel Club de Portugal	Lisbon	563931
Puerto Rico	Federacion de Automovilismo de Puerto Rice	San Juan	764-4271
Qatar	Auto & Touring Club of Qatar	Doha	22.734
Romania	Auto Club Roman	Bucharest	15-55-10
Senegal	Auto Club of Senegal	Dakar	348-21
Singapore	Auto Assoc. of Singapore	Singapore	73-22-444
South Africa	Auto Association of South Africa	Johannesburg Cape Town Pretoria	28-1400 21-1550 28-3829
Spain	Real Automovil Club de Espana	Madrid	447.32.00
Sri Lanka	Auto Assoc. of Ceylon	Colombo	215-28
Sweden	Motormannes Riksforbund	Stockholm	(08)670-580
Switzerland	Touring Club Suisse (TCS)	Geneva Basel Bern Lausanne Luzern Zurich	(022)37-12-12 (061)23-19-55 (031)44-22-22 (021)20-20-11 (041)23-78-33 (01)201-25-36
Syria	Auto Club of Syria	Damascus	220277
Thailand	Royal Auto Assoc.	Bangkok	511-22-30
Trinidad & Tobago	Trinidad & Tobago Auto Assn.	Port of Spain	62-27194
Tunisia	National Auto Club of Tunisia	Tunis	241.176
Turkey	Touring & Auto Club of Turkey	Istanbul	46-70-90
USSR	Federatzia Avtomobilnovo Sporta SSSR	Moscow	491.86.61
UAE	Automobile & Touring Club for UAE	Sharjah	23183
United States	*American Auto Association	Nationwide:	(800) 336-4357

Country	Name of Association	City	Telephone
Uruguay	Automovil Club del Uruguay	Montevideo	98.47.10
Venezuela	Touring y Automovil Club de Venezuela (TACV)	Caracus	(02)91.55.71
Yugoslavia	Auto-Moto-Savez Jugoslavije	Belgrade	(011)401-699
Zaire	Federation Automobile du Zaire	Kinshasha	
Zimbabwe	Auto Assoc. of Zimbabwe	Harare	70.70.21

*Asterisk denotes full reciprocity with American Automobile Association and Canadian Automobile Association.

Part Two
Driver's
Mechanical Manual

Chapter Fourteen: What You Should Always Keep in Your Car

You always should carry the following items in your car:

Safety Items

1. Lighting devices (flares, reflective triangles portable flashing lights, and a flashlight);
2. Light colored clothing;
3. Eye goggles;
4. A flag or sign;
5. CB radio or car telephone;
6. Chocks or blocks to keep car from moving;
7. Chains or traction devices;
8. Fire extinguisher;
9. First-aid kit (see chapter 21);

Personal Items

10. Extra keys;
11. Extra clothing, including walking shoes and a blanket;
12. Sunglasses;
13. Change for telephone;
14. Maps;
15. Water (drinkable) and food;

Automobile Repair Items

16. Spare tire, jack and lug wrench;
17. Jumper cables;
18. Extra fuses and light bulbs;
19. Tool kit and gauges;
20. Wear-out parts (belts);
21. Engine oil.

There are three basic priorities one must consider when stocking a car with these devices: safety needs, personal needs and the automobile's mechanical needs. In order of importance, we will deal with safety considerations first.

Safety Items

Whether it is day or night, whether your car is disabled or just parked, it is critically important that other motorists can see you and your car with enough lead time and distance for them to avoid hitting you or be caused to divert in an unsafe manner. Consequently, it is important to have some sort of device that is universally recognized and visible to catch the eye of surrounding traffic. The common red signal flare is such a device. A flare when lit produces a bright waivering light that can be seen in daylight as well as at night. You should carry enough flares to burn for 30 minutes or more.

Portable electric flashers and reflective triangles also are devices that can be used to detour traffic around your disabled car. These devices are less effective than flares but are reusable and safer to use. Light colored clothing and light reflective material are helpful in allowing others to see you outside your car. **Do not take for granted that oncoming traffic can see you.** Be careful: do not place yourself between oncoming traffic and your disabled car. Someone not realizing your car is disabled could easily pin you between the two cars.

In cold, snowy areas it would be of great convenience to carry chains for installation on the drive wheels when road conditions prevent sufficient traction. There are various types of chain devices that are made and the variety prevent me from specifically detailing their use. Read your owner's manual for suggestions as to the correct type and size of chain device. Since some cars are manufactured in such a way that fender clearance prevents the use of chains altogether, you must do a little research on what devices will safely add traction to the wheels of your car in adverse conditions. If your car is stuck, a shovel, sand, or a steel grate can be used to aide getting your car back onto a surface that will permit independent traction.

The next items to consider having for safety reasons are devices that either will aide in, or prevent, your car from moving.

In the event your brakes have failed or you must lift the wheels that the emergency brake locks, a portable device must be available to place in front and behind the remaining wheels to keep them from moving. Such a device is called a chock. A chock is a triangular block that can be wedged between the wheel and the ground to keep the wheel from rolling in that direction. Two chocks, one in front and one behind a grounded wheel, would be the minimum required to keep the car from moving on its own. Chocks can be purchased commercially and are suitably portable to be stored in your car. A couple of blocks of wood, $2'' \times 4'' \times 6$ inches long, would also make reasonable chocks. In a pinch, any large hard object will do the job; rocks, luggage, books. Remember, these items must be of sufficient size and strength to prevent the car from rolling over them.

The last group of safety items that one must consider carrying in one's car are devices that will aide you in getting assistance when your car is disabled. A flag or cloth tied to the antenna is recognized as a sign of distress. An actual sign posted on the car that says "SEND HELP" has obvious advantage. Lipstick writes very well on glass, and such a sign can be written directly on the window of the car. With the availability of Citizen Band radios (CB), it is now possible by two way radio contact to call for help using one of the monitored channels (usually channel 9) set aside for such emergencies. These radios are reasonably priced and readily available at many electronic outlets. These radios can be simply installed and are readily portable.

Personal Needs

As simple as it may seem, the most likely item to have to facilitate moving the car is a key. A spare key hidden in magnetic waterproof container in an unseen but easily retrievable place on the car can be an enormous benefit. It your car were disabled you could leave your car and call a towing service, tell them where your car is, and they could unlock the car and remove it from the roadway, without your having to be on the scene. If two different keys are necessary to operate your car, one for the doors and one for the ignition, make sure both are hidden. If a separate gas cap key is necessary, one should be made available—if not with the hidden keys at least in the glove box. Do not forget, even if the car will not start, an ignition key may be necessary just to unlock the steering mechanism in order to move the car.

A familiarity with the location where you are disabled is of utmost importance. You must be able to provide accurate information to anyone as to your location. This can be accomplished with good local maps, if you do not have a working knowledge of the area. If you must leave your car and look for a phone to call for help, obviously you will need change to make that call. And lastly, do not forget your interim mode of transportation is on foot, so make sure you have some footwear that will accommodate a comfortable hike to get assistance.

The next group of items you should consider carrying in your car relates to the needs of yourself and passengers. Your automobile provides an artificial, but hopefully comfortable, environment in which you can travel. Certain portable items can enhance these features. Sun glasses can provide a measure of comfort to reduce eye fatigue and to improve vision. Light, well ventilated shoes can reduce foot fatigue. Loose fitting clothes are substantially more comfortable in which to drive; as they allow better circulation while sitting for long periods. Liquid refreshments (non-alcoholic) and food can aid comfortable driving.

In the event the environmental system fails in the car or the car is disabled entirely, it is important to be able to provide a substitute environment for you and your passengers. In cold weather, you should consider carrying a blanket and extra clothing to protect all concerned whether they stay with or abandon the car. Rain gear also should be available to protect at least one person in the event the car becomes immobile. Obviously, you must consider the season of the year and the conditions for which to be prepared to maintain comfort during a trip.

In review, items to aide comfort and protect you from environmental breakdown during a trip are as follows:

1. Sun glasses
2. Loose-fitting clothing;
3. Comfortable shoes, light weight and ventilated;
4. Refreshments, food and drink;
5. Additional clothing and blankets; and
6. Rain protection.

Mechanical Emergency Items

This section discusses the items necessary for getting your car back on the road after you are forced to stop driving, or after you are stuck on the road.

A common cause of a car not starting is insufficient charge in the battery. This condition will prevent the starter motor from turning the engine over at a rate fast enough to have ignition. Jumper cables are devices that allow you to tap the energy resource of another car battery in order to get you started. The proper use of these cables will be explained in a following section.

Another common circumstance that may disable your car is a flat tire. The proper tools necessary to lift the flat tire off the ground and remove it from the car should be available with you. These include a usable tire to take the place of a damaged tire. The proper use of a jack, lug wrench and spare tire will be explained in a following chapter.

There are many electrical systems on all cars and they are protected from overloading by fuses. One fuse may protect a number of items within a system and one malfunctioning item will cause an entire system to shut down. Consequently, it would be wise to carry extra fuses to enable you to put a system back in service by a simple replacement. Once replacing that fuse, test the operation of all the items that may appear on the fuse network. If the use of one item (i.e., headlights) blows the new fuse, replace the fuse again and refrain from use of the damaged item until you can get service. If all system items appear to work without blowing the new fuse, you may proceed without service. It is quite likely that the fuse has fatigued, and no system problem exists.

Gauges

Gauges allow you to monitor the functioning of your car to prevent roadside emergencies. Some gauges are portable and some I consider important enough to be installed as permanent features in the car. It is important to be able to meter the critical systems of your car while operating or parked. Your car is manufactured with some of these, but in some cases all you are provided with is an indicator (idiot) light that just tells when a system has failed. These are used specifically to indicate when there is no oil pressure or that the motor has overheated. These are not good monitors of these systems. Often they tell you of problems when it is too late to prevent damage to the car or, minimally, at which point you should no longer drive the car. You have been provided no opportunity to witness changes in the systems as they function. Consequently, I recommend the installation of gauges. With gauges you can see system fluctuations, and with the knowledge of the systems operating specifications, you can make decisions about their conditions.

Most automobile manufacturers provide gauges either as standard equipment or as an option. If not, there is a large aftermarket trade that will provide standard gauge sets that may be installed into virtually any car. At least, you should have gauges that tell you the amount of oil pressure that is being developed within the motor and the operating temperature of the motor. A voltage meter also is recommended. It can tell the condition of the battery and output of the charging system under operating conditions.

Certain portable gauges are also useful. A tire pressure gauge allows you to conveniently monitor the air pressure in your tires, including the spare. A thermometer, similar to a meat thermometer, tells you the temperature of your coolant in the radiator or the temperature coming out of your air conditioning ducts. Both of these devices are readily available at automobile supply stores.

Wear-Out Parts

It maybe advisable to carry an assortment of "wear-out parts" with you on a trip. To chose these parts, you must be able to categorize their need by a priority system. First are items that are friction materials that continually wear in use; brake pads; brake shoes; rubber parts, such as belts and hoses; ignition parts, such as points, spark plugs, condensors, distributor cap and rotor; and filters—oil, air and fuel.

Second it is wise to know the availability of these parts. This can only be determined by a little research. Know the make, model and year of production of your car. Determine how popular a model it is by discussions with service facilities. If many of these cars are still on the road, parts should be readily available. Some cars or models of cars have been marketed in specific areas and parts availability will vary with geography.

Third, consider the actual possibility of needing various parts on the road. If certain parts have been replaced recently and their life span is two years, it may not be necessary to carry a spare.

Finally, having a part may not mean it is possible to change it on the road, or that you have the ability to do so. Consequently, carrying a lot of wear out parts in your trunk will not assure a positive benefit.

Some examples might go like this. You own a late model, domestic sedan that is a common family car throughout the country. It might be wise to carry a set of belts, and maybe a couple of the larger hoses. If any of those failed on the road, you could probably change them on the road. Local parts availability would make it unnecessary to carry many more specific parts.

If you own an older, limited-edition car, or an import with a limited dealership network, it maybe advisable to carry many of the "wear-out" parts to facilitate any service professional getting you back on the road promptly.

Carrying many parts in your car is rarely beneficial because there are too many reasons for a car to fail and your having the tools and expertise to determine the reason for failure is not realistic.

Tool Kit Items

Your tool kit should include screwdrivers (phillips, flathead, and torx), an adjustable wrench or a socket set, a hammer, work gloves, rags, flashlight, and a variety of mending staples. A knife, scraper and a wire-cutter can come in handy; however a single-edged razor blade will suffice for cutting wire or scraping. Sandpaper or steel wool is useful for cleaning battery terminals or other surfaces.

There are certain universal mending staples that could help you out in a more general sense. A roll of electrical tape can be used to mend a hose or wire. A roll of radiator hose tape is very good for temporarily sealing leaks. A length of wire of sufficient thickness can be used to replace a cable or even a belt. A quart of motor oil and a gallon of water could help renew those fluid levels enough to get you back on the road. I recommend bringing water which is potable so that you can drink it if you are stranded.

Chapter Fifteen: Warning Signs: When You Should Not Drive Any Further

This chapter will describe warning signs which will indicate that your safety is in danger, or your vehicle is in jeopardy of being severely damaged. There are nine major warning signs:

1. Braking abnormalities;
2. Steering abnormalities;
3. Electrical problems;
4. Engine signals;
5. Leaks;
6. Overheating.
7. Noises;
8. Smells; and
9. Vibrations.

Safety

Safety is the first factor that I take into consideration when deciding if a car should be driven. If at any time you feel you cannot safely control the car, it is imperative that you stop immediately. The most important control aspect of the car is the ability to stop. If there is an unusual feel about the braking of the car, the car swerves when braking, the pedal feels soft or goes down too close to the floor, or if there are peculiar noises when the pedal is depressed, you must refrain from driving the car. Some symptoms do not render the car unsafe to drive, but unless you can determine this as a fact, never take the chance. Have the car towed to your service professional.

Being able to accurately steer your car is the next important safety consideration. If you feel an abnormal amount of play or looseness in the steering wheel, your ability to control your car is severely compromised. Hard spots in the steering can mean you are headed for a steering system seizure, a very dangerous situation. Vibrations and noises transmitted through the steering column may not indicate a serious mechanical problem but severe vibrations will make the car difficult to steer. Once again, the severity of these problems will dictate how safe the car is to drive, but if there is any question, do not take the chance. Seek help in making that determination or play it safe and have the car towed to where it can be serviced.

Less obviously, the inability to accelerate and keep up with traffic around you is a dangerous condition. A severe loss of engine power or the ability to transmit that power to the wheels must be considered as a safety issue.The severity of this problem will dictate the need for a tow, or a direct detour to the repair shop.

The ability to see or be seen at night is an important safety consideration. If your lights do not work or there is a question of the ability of your car to provide enough illumination, do not drive the car. Pull over to the side of the road, or to a service station. If your bright lights work, but your headlights do not, use your brights, but avoid blinding oncoming traffic. If your rear lights are not working, try your emergency flashers. Make sure that you check your fuses, look for a disconnected wire, or install a new bulb if available.

Engine Condition

The next group of conditions that should prevent you from driving any further have to do with real or perceived engine faults. If you notice a leak of any of the critical fluids (water, oil, gasoline) the car should not be driven until the severity of that leak can be determined.

Motor oil lubricates virtually all of the moving parts within the engine. An inadequate amount or inadequate pressure, determined by a gauge, should be immediate cause for you to pull over and shut off the engine. If there is a leak of a minor nature that allows you to keep sufficient oil in the engine for a period, you may drive the car to a service center. If there is insufficent oil pressure, even though the oil level is proper, do not drive the car. You could magnify the damage by using the car any further.

Water, or a water and antifreeze mixture, is the fluid that is circulated through the engine block and radiator to draw off excess heat. A loss of this coolant will make it impossible for the cooling system to carry away this heat. The metal moving parts inside the engine were designed to operate within a certain temperature range. Once you exceed this range those metal parts will expand or deform to sizes incompatible with the connecting parts with which they were designed to operate. Consequently, a seizure is imminent. If your car runs hot or overheats, which can be determined by a gauge, do not drive it any further.

Gasoline leaks are particularly dangerous because, if given an opportunity, gasoline will burn on the outside of your engine as well as it does within. There are many devices on your engine that will provide the spark or heat necessary to ignite leaking gasoline. If you smell gas or see it leaking do not drive the car and do not smoke near it.

The engine drives a number of devices as well as the wheels. To provide electrical power for the ignition system, the starting system, battery and auxiliary systems (lights, blower, radio, etc.), the engine turns, via a belt, an alternator or generator. This device has moving parts that can fail. When it does, electrical power is not being generated, and once the stored electrical power within the battery is consumed, the car will not run. Consequently, if the charging system voltage is insufficient, which can be determined by a gauge, you should not drive the car because you are in danger of becoming disabled with little warning.

Look, Listen, Feel and Smell

Other reasons for considering not driving your car will be based upon what you perceive by your innate human senses: what you see, hear, feel and smell. If you feel vibrations under the car of an indeterminate nature, you should not drive the car. Such vibrations may be the precursor of a wheel bearing letting loose, a drive shaft universal joint breaking, a transmission giving out or any drive line part on the verge of failure.

If you see a worn out or flat tire your decision to drive becomes very easy. If you hear unusual noises from the brakes or any part of the car that you feel is not normal, you should consider not driving the car or at least just enough to seek a professional opinion.

If you smell any burning odor around your car, you must try to determine its origin. An electrical malfunction, a fan belt trying to turn a seized water pump, brake seizure, oil dripping on a hot exhaust pipe and many other circumstances can cause burning smells, and most are cause to prevent your from driving any further. Leaking gasoline has it s own definite odor and the risk of explosion and fire is severe. A rotten-egg type odor may be a sign that the battery is being overcharged. This circumstance is also very dangerous because the gas that the battery emits is explosive when a spark is present. Use your senses and good common sense when making the judgment "should I drive this car any further?"

Chapter Sixteen:
Check List for a Trip

If you routinely maintain your car it should routinely take you where you want to go. There is a check list you should follow in order to prepare you and your car for a long trip. Know the maintenance schedule of your car and have the next closest scheduled maintenance performed before your trip. Know you car well enough so you can perceive any abnormalities or deficencies and have them corrected during this maintenance. An idea of your optimal gas mileage is good to know, because you can judge the need for a tune up, or other service if your car is not meeting or exceeding that figure.

You can divide your check list into five categories as follows:

1. Under the Hood

■ **Check all fluid levels:**
- ☐ battery water level
- ☐ radiator water/antifreeze
- ☐ windshield washer
- ☐ engine oil
- ☐ transmission/clutch oil
- ☐ power steering fluid
- ☐ brake fluid

■ **Check rubber parts:**
- ☐ belts
- ☐ hoses

■ **Check electrical parts:**
　□ check and clean battery terminals
　□ check for loose, broken or frayed wiring
■ **Check for loose bolts, screws and other hardware.**

2. Inside the Car

■ **Check rubber friction pads on brake, clutch and gas pedals**
■ **Start engine to determine whether gauges are working**
■ **Check operation of all systems:**
　□ lights
　□ horn
　□ emergency flashers
　□ turn signals
　□ windshield wipers

3. Outside the Car

■ Check all lights (it helps to have an assistant to check brake lights)
■ Check for loose trim
■ Check wiper blades
■ Check and tighten license plates
■ Check tires for proper pressure, wear and damage

4. In the Trunk

■ Check spare tire
■ Check tool kit
■ Check list in chapter 14 (what you should always keep in your car)

5. Under the Car

■ Check exhaust system for leaks, noise and loose connections
■ Check differential oil level
■ Check for leaks
■ Check for loose parts

Under the Hood

Learn how to check your own car. If you can't find the dipstick, for example, look in your owner's manual. Know where everything is supposed to be and how it is supposed to look.

You should check visually all the rubber parts for cracks, bulges and unusual wear. These include the hoses, fan belt and other belts. Check all fluid levels and conditions. The fluids include motor oil, transmission oil, brake fluid, clutch hydraulic fluid (if applicable), power steering fluid, (if applicable), coolant level and percentage of antifreeze, air conditioning freon, battery water and windshield washer fluid. You can check most of these fluids by yourself. Check with your owner's manual for the directions that explain how to check these various fluid levels.

Your battery should be thoroughly checked. Some of the newer "freedom" batteries are sealed and therefore you cannot add water to them. However even a fully charged battery can cause problems if the connections are not good. Battery terminals corrode. Disconnect the post and terminals and clean them with a stiff brush, steel wool or sandpaper. You can use a solution of baking soda and water. When cleaned, tightly reconnect the terminals.

Look for loose wiring, frayed wires, loose parts and connections. If something looks wrong check with a service professional.

Inside the Car

Check the brake pedal movement and try to determine if the free travel is not excessive. Look at the rubber friction pads on all of your pedals to see if they are badly worn. Replace them if worn or missing. Start your engine and make sure all of your gauges are operating properly. Check your horn, lights, emergency flashers, turn signals and windshield wipers. Try the windshield washer and make sure the wiper blades are cleaning the windows. Replace wiper blades if they are worn, or streaking the windows.

Outside the Car

Do a visual check of all lights. It is easier to check the lights if you have a helper. Make sure that you check out the brake lights. Look for loose trim and tighten your license plates. Check your owner's manual for proper tire inflation. Check your tires for air pressure, uneven wear, cuts, breaks or blisters. If your tires are worn unevenly your wheel alignment should be checked. If your spare tire is in better condition than your tires, use it to replace the worst tire. You should not drive with less than 1/16th of an inch of tread. You can use a U.S. penny to check the tread depth. If the tread is deeper than President Lincoln's head, you have enough tread. If not, replace the tire, because it is unsafe and illegal.

In the Trunk

Look over your spare tire and check its air pressure. Make sure that it is tightly secured in the trunk. Check your tool kit and first aid kits. Make sure that you have everything on the list included in chapter 14.

Under the Car

If you feel uncomfortable under your car have a service professional check for you. Your exhaust system should be checked for leaks. This can be done by turning on your engine and then stuffing a rag into the exhaust pipe. If there are leaks you will see exhaust gases coming out of a hole in a pipe or the muffler. Check for oil leaks, loose parts and fittings. Check the differential oil level.

Take a Test Ride

On a trip you may have to carry a substantial load, including suitcases and additional passengers. Since this may not be a normal circumstance for your car, load the car with additional weight and see if it feels peppy enough and stops safely.

All long trips should be preceeded by a short shake-down ride in order to make sure you feel confident with the condition of the car. This should occur with enough lead time before the trip to allow you to get any deficiency corrected and retested before leaving. Remember, most good repair shops are busy and require appointments and lead time for repairs. Emergency repairs should not proceed long trips because such repairs are frequently not permanent.

Know your car's track record. Record all your service information so you can chart the deterioration of the various mechanical systems. A car is a piece of machinery that essentially consumes itself in use. Being current on the available life of particular parts is essential. A three-year-old battery is probably, depending on its rating, near the end of its life. Brake pads with 40,000 miles on them may also be at the end of their use. If you can document the span of use of various parts, a service professional will be able to make a valuable judgment that may prevent you from being disabled on the road. In general, the older the car, the greater the probability you will be stranded on the road. Know the frequency of repairs of your particular make and model as documented by **Consumer Reports** magazine, ask your mechanic for advice about your car. This compiled information may help you decide what additional maintenance may be necessary, or whether to consider alternative transportation if too many questionable circumstances are present.

Chapter Seventeen: How to Handle Mechanical Emergencies

If your car overheats, runs out of gas, gets a flat tire, or otherwise should not be driven, pull as far off the roadway as possible. Changing tires and working on a car on the highway is a major cause of highway fatalities.

Place a series of flares to give traffic warning that you are disabled. If you don't have flares use portable flashing lights. Portable electric flashers and reflective triangles are less effective than flares, but are reusable and safer to use. In any event use your emergency flashers, wear light-colored clothing and/or reflective material. Do not place yourself between oncoming traffic and the disabled vehicle.

Raise the hood of your car, and hang a white cloth or flag on the antenna or driver's door. This is the international distress signal. If you need assistance and have a citizens band radio, call for help on channel nine or 19.

How to Use Flares

Extreme care must be used when using flares. Before lighting the flare check the area where it is to be used. Be certain that your car and nearby vehicles are not leaking gasoline or other flammable liquids. Wet spots on the road, not identifiable as water, can ignite. Protect your hands and face, especially your eyes, when lighting a flare. Place the lighted flare sufficiently far enough behind your car, and near the roadway, to allow traffic to avoid hitting the vehicle. The speed of traffic, curves in the roadway and obstructions will determine where, the number and location of flares that you should use.

Make sure that all flares are extinguished before leaving the area. The lighted end of the flare should be snuffed into the ground and then disposed of properly. The unburned part can cause harm and the wire holder can puncture tires.

Chapter Eighteen: How to Change a Tire

Read in your owner's manual to determine the correct manner for using your jack. Jacks are designed to lift the weight of one wheel and have not been designed to withstand lateral movement. Therefore it is critical that you supply additional means to prevent the car from moving sideways, forward or backward. Follow these steps:

1. Roll or drive your car to a safe location for jacking. A safe location is one that is level, off the roadway or as far to the curb as possible and unobstructed;

2. Lay out all the necessary tools and spare tire, including the jack and handle, lug wrench, screwdriver, wheel chocks or blocks;

3. Secure car to prevent rolling. Set the handbrake, put in gear if your car has a standard transmission, or in park if an automatic. Place wheel chocks in front and behind of the wheel that will remain on the ground and is on the same side of the car as the wheel to be removed;

4. Remove hub cap and loosen the lug nuts one turn before jacking the car;

5. Jack the wheel off the ground;

6. Remove lug nuts and place them inside the hub cap;

7. Remove flat tire and place under the car, near the jack. This will protect you and the car if the jack fails;

8. Put the spare tire on the car and install lug nuts with your hands (do not tighten with a wrench);

9. Remove flat tire beneath car;

10. Lower the jack until tire touches the ground. Tighten lug nuts with the wrench;

11. Lower the jack completely and remove;

12. Remove chocks;

13. Visually check the new tire to make sure it is not flat;

14. Get the damaged tire repaired or replaced as soon as possible.

SAFETY NOTE: Never place any part of your body under a car that is on a jack without first placing some object between the ground and the car to prevent the car from pinning you in case the jack fails.

Chapter Nineteen: What To Do When Your Car Won't Start

There are four basic reasons why your car is not starting:

1. Insufficient cranking power;
2. No spark or poor spark;
3. No fuel or poor fuel; or
4. Inadequate compression.

Of course, more than one of these factors could be acting together, so if you find one problem and correct it, your car might still not start.

Cranking is the ability of the starter motor to turn the engine at a sufficient rate so compression occurs and fuel is drawn into the combustion chamber. The parts that relate to cranking are the ignition switch, battery, starter motor and the charging system (alternator).

Spark is created by spark plugs, ignition or high-tension cables, distributor cap and rotor, points and condensor (in a non-transistorized ignition system), pick-up, magnet and amplifier (in a transistorized ignition), and a coil.

Fuel is brought to the combustion chamber by the fuel pump, fuel lines, filter and gas tank.

Compression is caused by the movement of the pistons in their cylinders.

Knowing these basic terms and parts is important to an understanding of the four basic systems. A working knowledge of their functions is not critical, but the more educated you are the better the decision that you can make regarding proper service. When you are more informed you can give a mechanic more accurate facts about the condition of your car.

Crank

If your car will not turn over or crank you can try to start it by:

1. Checking the battery connections. Remove the cables from the battery posts and scrape the contact surfaces with a knife or rolled-up piece of sandpaper. Reconnect the cables tightly.

2. If you still can't start the car you can "jump-start" it from the battery of another car, or by means of a battery charger. I will describe how to jump-start your car in chapter twenty.

3. If you are unable to jump-start the car, your car can be pushed or rolled to get it started. This can be done only if you have a standard transmission and a certain expertise. I do not recommend this procedure unless you are trained, or have the assistance of a professional.

4. The last resort is to have the car towed to a service station.

Spark

If your car does turn over or crank, but still won't start, check to see if sufficient spark is being produced. Pull one ignition wire off any spark plug. Hold the disconnected wire about one-half inch from the engine block. Be careful doing this because you can be shocked. Don't conduct this test near water, and make sure that you are wearing gloves and wearing rubber-soled shoes. Have someone turn the ignition key so that the engine will turn over. You should be able to observe a bright blue spark jump from the end of the ignition wire to the engine block. If you do not see this you probably have an ignition problem. When you have diagnosed this problem, most likely you will not be able to repair it on the road. A tow to the garage is the next step.

Fuel

If you have a good spark, next check the fuel system. All you can really determine on the road is whether fuel is being supplied to the carburetor or fuel injector. This can be accomplished by removing the fuel line that enters the carburetor and having someone turn the key. When the engine turns over, fuel should spew out of the line. Be prepared with a container to catch the fuel. If no fuel is coming out make sure there is fuel in your tank. If there is fuel in your tank, but it isn't coming through the fuel line, you will have to have the car towed to a repair shop.

Compression

If you are getting a good spark, good fuel flow and the car still will not start, you may have a compression problem. In this event it is unlikely that any road service will get you started.

Chapter Twenty: How to Jump-Start Your Car Safely

Jump-starting a car is a procedure to get your car started when your battery has insufficient power to start the engine. It requires the use of another vehicle with a fully-charged battery, or a battery charger.

In order to connect the electrical systems of two cars you will need a pair of jumper cables. They are thick cables with large spring clamps on either end. To jump-start a car:

1. Bring the operative car as close to the disabled car as possible so that the cables will reach between the batteries;

2. Put on eye goggles to protect your eyes. Batteries can explode. Attach one of the cables, the one with red clamps, if marked, between the red, or positive (+) terminal on each battery;

3. Start the operative car;

4. Attach the second jumper cable [black clamps (–)], between the negative terminal of the operative car and a metal part of the disabled car. **DO NOT CONNECT** the cable to the negative post of the disabled car's battery because you may cause a spark when the connection is made or broken. This spark could ignite the hydrogen gas that is produced by the battery when charging. This spark could cause the battery to explode and spew acid over you and your car;

5. Let the operative car run for a few minutes with the cables connected before trying to start the disabled car. This allows the dead battery to absorb some charge;

6. Start the disabled car. If the disabled car turns over at a sufficient rate of speed, the car should start fairly quickly. If it does not, do not continue to crank endlessly because you evidently have another problem;

7. After the car has started, keep the cables connected for a few minutes, then disconnect the black (or negative) cable from the frame of the disabled car. Then disconnect the other side of the negative cable. Disconnect the red or positive cable from both batteries and put the cables away;

8. Allow the disabled car to run for a few minutes on its own power to insure that the charging system is functioning properly. If you have a voltmeter gauge in your car, you can see if the battery is recharging. If the battery is not holding a charge, you may need a new battery. As soon as possible have your battery and charging system checked.

Chapter Twenty-One: Towing Your Car

Towing your car is a job for a professional. Usually you should not attempt to tow a car on your own. Cars should be towed with proper hook ups to the frame or suspension. There are a number of differing towing mechanisms that may or may not be suitable for your car. Your owner's manual will give you specific towing instructions.

The most common type of towing equipment is the **sling tow.** This lifts two wheels off the ground, front or back, and allows the weight of the car to be distributed upon the other two wheels. Some bumpers and underbody parts cannot carry this extra weight, so great care must be exercised. If possible the drive wheels should be held up by the sling. If not possible the drive wheels should be placed on a dolly.

Crane towing and **flat-bed towing** have less risk of damage. However, they are more expensive methods of towing. Flat-bed towing is the best since the entire car is loaded onto the back of a flat-bed trailer.

Chapter Twenty-Two: Opening a Frozen Door Lock

Frozen door locks are caused by moisture, which freezes when trapped in the locking mechanism. To prevent frozen locks you can inject commercially available chemicals into the lock.

To unlock a frozen door you can:

- Heat the key with a match or lighter;
- Use a hair dryer;
- Use a deicing product;

I do not recommend using hot water, even though it will work temporarily. Introducing more water to the lock will only lead to refreezing. **Do not use an open flame** as it may damge the finish on your car, or ruin the lock. Lastly, a little sunshine can cure this problem.

Chapter Twenty-Three: What To Do When Your Car Overheats

When your car overheats you should move the car to a safe place immediately and shut off the engine. Just driving to the next exit, or a few miles down the road, can make the difference between a minor water leak and a destroyed engine. Raise the hood, both to allow the heat to rise away from the car, and to signify to other motorists that you are disabled. **Do not remove the radiator cap for at least 15 minutes.** A great deal of pressure can develop in a hot "cooling" system, and removing the cap can cause scalding coolant to be sprayed all over you.

After waiting, put on a pair of work gloves (or use a rag) and turn the cap slowly to bleed off air pressure. Once the air pressure has been released, remove the cap. If the water level is low, or not visible, add water or antifreeze solution until the system is full. Look for leaking hoses. If a hose has a leak, or a clamp has loosened, you can make an emergency repair by tightening the clamp, or by using electrical or radiator hose tape. Make sure that the fan is working. If the fan is an electric fan and is not working, check for loose connections and check the proper fuse. Use your owner's manual to determine which fuse is on the fan's circuit.

If, after filling the system, there are no apparent symptoms of overheating, steam or boiling over, put the cap back on and drive to the nearest service station. Watch the engine temperature closely and stop again if the temperature gets dangerously high.

In cars with expansion tanks (plastic reservoirs connected to the radiator), looking at the tank will not necessarily tell you if there is enough fluid in the radiator. The radiator may be empty even though the expansion tank is not. Pour additional water into the expansion tank and see if the water is used in the radiator.

If you cannot determine the source of the problem and correct it, call for a tow truck.

Chapter Twenty-Four: What To Do When the Lights Go Out

If you have noticed one light out, it is safe to assume that the bulb has burned out. If the lowbeam on a headlight does not work, but the highbeam does, the light probably needs to be replaced. If a series of lights are out (both brake lights, for example), it is likely that a fuse needs to be replaced.

If bulb and fuse replacement do not correct the problem, things can get quite complicated. A loose wire may be the problem. Or it could be one of twenty other things.

If you are stranded at night on a highway, drive only if other cars can see you. You may have to use your emergency flashers, or your highbeams, to be seen. But it is better to use alternate lighting than to freeze to death, or be stranded for long periods on a deserted highway. Use your common sense. Borrow light bulbs from non-essential uses. If your brake light bulbs have burned out, use one from the trunk of your car, or from an interior light.

Part Three
Driver's First Aid Manual

Driver's First-Aid Manual

Introduction

This part of the book is designed to aid the occupants of an automobile who are having a medical emergency. Nearly every medical need imaginable can arise in your car. I have discussed only the most common problems, and those most likely to occur in an automobile accident.

Medical problems are provided in an alphabetical list of chapters starting with back and neck injuries (Chapter 27) to seizures (Chapter 40). Each chapter is concise so that it can be referred to in case of emergency. However, you should familiarize yourself with this material before you have a crisis. A list of these chapters is reprinted below.

Chapter 25 includes a list of items that you should keep in your first-aid kit. Chapter 26 explains how you should decide which victims should be treated first.

Medical Emergencies

27. BACK & NECK INJURIES.
28. BLEEDING.
29. BROKEN BONES (FRACTURES).
30. CARBON MONOXIDE POISONING.
31. CARDIOVASCULAR RESUSCITATION (CPR.)

32. CARSICKNESS.
33. CHEST INJURIES.
34. DIABETES
35. DROWSINESS—WARNING SIGNS
    TO STOP DRIVING.
36. EYE INJURIES.
37. HEAD INJURIES.
38. HEART ATTACK.
39. NAUSEA & VOMITING.
40. PREGNANCY.
41. SEIZURES.
42. SNOWBOUND SURVIVAL

Chapter Twenty-Five: Your First-Aid Kit

An emergency first-aid kit should be prepared for your car and kept inside the car, rather than in the trunk. It should be kept inside the car, either in the glove compartment or on the rear shelf, because an accident may trap you inside the car, or jam the trunk shut.

Commercially-made kits are available, but supplies easily can be assembled by the car owner. If you buy a ready-made first-aid kit make sure that it contains all essential items.

Your emergency first-aid kit should include:

■ gauze bandages in rolls and individual packages;

■ ace wraps;

■ slings;

■ cotton swabs;

■ antiseptic cream;

■ medical tape;

■ scissors;

■ pain reliever;

■ nausea remedy; and

■ flash light.

Chapter Twenty-Six: Priorities of Treatment

When an accident occurs, and more than one person is injured, a rapid screening (triage) of the victims must take place. Those in most distress must receive immediate attention. In addition, the motor vehicle must be assessed as to possible risk of fire or explosion. (This only infrequently occurs, except on television). Risk of fire or explosion would certainly modify your efforts to attend to the victims.

If there is risk of fire or explosion all victims must be removed from the vehicle as quickly as possible. Any victim suspected of having a neck or back injury must be handled with proper splinting. Chapter 27 on back and neck injuries should be reviewed for moving these victims. Before abandoning a vehicle make sure that the ignition is turned off.

Assuming that fire or explosion is not imminent, I suggest that your priorities should be:

1. Unconscious persons;
2. Open wounds of the chest;
3. Severe bleeding;
4. Back and neck injuries; and
5. Broken bones.

Chapter Twenty-Seven: Back and Neck Injuries

Back and neck (spine) injuries can be severe and are potentially disastrous. Consequently, they must be treated by skilled hands. If at all possible the best course of action is to **avoid movement of the injured person.** The victim must be assessed to determine if there is a spine injury, and the extent of the injury.

Signs and Symptoms

The following are signs and symptoms of spine injury:

■ Pain along the spine;

■ Tenderness to touch;

■ Apprehension as to motions of the spine;

■ Inability to move arms or legs;

■ Numbness or "pins and needles" sensation in arms or legs;

■ Loss of bladder or bowel control; and

■ Difficulty with breathing.

Course of Action

Always assume that there is a spine injury unless the victim can tell you otherwise. If an injured person is having difficulty breathing, keep him or her lying down, and slightly tilt the head backwards. This must be done very gently because to rough a movement could cause paralysis or death. If the victim is facedown, he must be logrolled as a unit. Any twisting of the spine could cause further neurologic damage.

If there is nausea and vomiting, the patient should be on his side to prevent choking. He must be logrolled onto his side. The patient should be splinted, and then stabilized with rocks, towels, blankets or clothing on the sides of the head and body.

Splinting

Neck

Any motion must be made with extreme caution. Any motion must be **axial,** with the victim moving as a unit. Place a board beneath the shoulders to above the head and secure the patient with tape or straps.

If no board is available, wrap towels, clothing or newspaper about the head and neck. Avoid wrapping the windpipe.

Back

Keep the patient in whatever position he is found, unless he is facedown in water, or has facial injuries. If the victim must be moved use the logrolling technique. To logroll a person safely place a board under him and move him as a unit.

If the patient is unconscious, he should be placed on his side to keep the windpipe from being obstructed.

When the patient is on his back, he should be lifted as a unit, from the head and shoulders and the board slid beneath him. Alternatively, the victim can be rolled carefully to the side, and then back over the board.

If a victim has to be moved, make sure that you have help so that the move can be effected smoothly. **Do not move a patient unless absolutely necessary, and do not move a patient unless you know what you are doing.**

Chapter Twenty-Eight: Bleeding

When there is bleeding, the extent of blood loss must be assessed promptly. Superficial wounds in areas of rich blood supply (for example, the scalp), may seem worse than they really are. Internal injuries to the chest or abdomen may not show any external signs of blood loss, but can quickly lead to shock and death.

Bleeding can be either from arteries or veins. Arterial bleeding pulses from the wound and is a bright red color. Venous bleeding is characterized by constant flow and is dark red.

Treatment

Direct Pressure

Direct pressure is the foremost method of controlling hemorrhage. The direct pressure method is as follows:

1. Place a gauze pad, or other piece of cloth, directly on the wound, and apply constant pressure;

2. If the cloth or pad becomes saturated with blood, apply a second or third layer over the first, rather than removing a layer;

3. Elevate the area of bleeding above the level of the heart, unless a fracture is suspected. This will lessen the blood flow to the wound;

4. After the bleeding slows or stops, wrap an ace bandage or folded sling directly over the existing gauze or cloth.

Pressure Points

Pressure points is a technique which is used only for bleeding that cannot be controlled by direct pressure and elevation. It is designed to decrease or stop blood flow to the wound at the blood vessel feeding that area.

Arm

The presssure point technique for a bleeding arm: using your fingers, grasp the inside of the arm midway between the elbow and the shoulder. Apply a counterforce on the outside of the arm and your thumb. Apply constant, firm pressure while maintaining elevation of the arm above the heart.

Leg

To use the pressure point technique for a bleeding leg the victim must be lying down on his back. Place the heel of your hand on the mid portion of the leg at the groin crease. Apply constant, firm pressure until the bleeding stops or slows.

Tourniquet

A **tourniquet** should be used only as a last resort. It has fallen into disfavor because the technique itself can cause considerable damage. For this technique apply a wide cloth (between two and four inches) above the arm or leg were the bleeding is occurring. A men's neck tie, or a scarf can be used. Tie a half-knot. Place a stick or other straight object across the knot and tie another knot. Twist the stick until bleeding slows or stops. Note the time of application—this can be written on the patient's forehead with pen or lipstick.

The tourniquet must remain in place until the patient reaches professional assistance. Do not cover the tourniquet: it must be noted immediately be a doctor or paramedic.

Hemorrhage-Causing Shock

The signs of a victim suffering from hemorrhage-causing shock are:
- cold, clammy or pale skin;
- weak and rapid pulse;
- restlessness;
- confusion;
- difficulty in breathing.

Treat a patient suffering from bleeding-induced shock by:

1. Keeping the patient lying down;
2. Elevating the person's legs unless fracture is considered;
3. Covering patient with a blanket or towels;
4. Maintaining an open airway so patient can breath;
5. Turning patient's head to side.

Internal Bleeding

Signs of internal bleeding are:
- Difficulty in breathing;
- Coughing up blood;
- Vomiting blood or coffee-ground appearing substance;

- Stools with blood or appearing black;
- Blood in urine;
- Signs of shock.

Treatment for internal bleeding:
1. Keep victim calm and lying down;
2. Don't give food or drink to person;
3. Seek professional assistance.

Chapter Twenty-Nine: Broken Bones (Fractures)

The most common type of fracture is a closed fracture, one that does not break through the skin. Open fractures are broken bones which penetrate the skin, and are far more likely to cause infection.

Signs of Broken Bones

Signs that a person suffered a fracture are:
- Obvious deformity;
- Tenderness or pain;
- Swelling;
- Pain on movement;
- Inability to move the injured area;
- Victim's description of a "snap" or grating sensation.

Treatment

1. Treat bleeding with direct pressure;
2. **Do not attempt to straighten the limb.**
3. **Do not push back any exposed bone.**
4. Cover any exposed area with a gauze bandage or clean cloth after cutting away the victim's clothing;
5. Apply splint.

Splinting

Splints are designed to reduce pain, control bleeding and facilitate transport. Splints are used for fractures in the arm, leg, fingers, toes, hand and foot. Any firm substance can be used: stiff cardboard, a stick, a rolled-up magazine or newspaper, or an umbrella. The splint should be secured well above and below the fracture. A pillow or blanket can be wrapped around the site of the injury and secured with tape, a rolled sling, rope, a belt, a scarf or necktie. **Do not fasten the splint so tightly that circulation is impaired.** This would be evident by swelling, numbness, or a bluish color of the skin distal to the splint. Distal means that part of the arm or leg situated away from the body and toward the fingers or toes.

Shoulder Injuries

When fractures of the shoulder area are suspected, keep the arm at the patient's side. Wrap an ace bandage or cloth around the arm and chest together. The body acts as a splint.

Upper Arm

Treat upper-arm fractures by wrapping a newspaper or magazine around the arm. Then secure the arm to the chest with an ace bandage.

Forearm and Wrist

Wrap a newspaper, magazine or blanket around the forearm and wrist. Then place the limb across the chest and use a sling (or make one out of cloth or a towel) to support it.

Elbow

Maintain the position of the elbow. **Do not manipulate any elbow injury,** as circulatory or nerve damage could result. Wrap a newspaper, magazine, blanket or towel around the elbow. Secure the elbow to the body with an ace bandage or tie.

Hand

Wrap a towel, newspaper, magazine or blanket around the wrist and hand, and secure with tape. Use a sling, if available. If a sling is not available fashion on with a towel, sheet or piece of cloth.

Hip

Secure legs together with rope, tape, or a necktie. A soft substance, such as a pillow, should be placed between the knees. The good leg acts as a splint for the one that is injured. Obviously, don't put any weight on the legs. Carry the victim on a stretcher if movement is necessary.

Thigh

Find a piece of wood, an umbrella or a tree limb for use as a splint. Secure the splint well above and below the location of the injury. If a splint is unavailable, secure the injured leg to the uninjured one with a pad between the knees. The uninjured leg will serve as a splint.

Knee

Place the entire leg on a board. Secure the leg well above and below the knee with tape or an ace bandage. Move the leg only as an entire unit.

Lower Leg

Find a piece of wood, an umbrella or other splint and secure it to the injured leg. If a splint is unavailable, wrap the lower leg in a blanket, pillow or newspaper.

Ankle or Foot

Find a pillow or blanket. Place ankle and foot on pillow or blanket and fold around the injured area. Secure the pillow with a rope, necktie or scarf.

Neck and Back

Spinal fractures can be very severe. Fractures of the spine can cause paralysis and death and must be attended to meticulously. See chapter twenty-seven for back and neck injuries.

Chapter Thirty: Carbon Monoxide Poisoning

Carbon monoxide, an odorless and deadly gas, is contained in automobile exhaust. In moving vehicles without leaks in the exhaust system, carbon monoxide poisoning will not take place. However, if there is a leak in the exhaust system, carbon monoxide poisoning will not take place. However, if there is a leak in your exhaust system, or you are parked in the car with the engine running, caution should be exercised.

Symptoms

Typical symptoms of carbon monoxide poisoning are:

■ Drowsiness;
■ Loss of consciousness;
■ Cherry-red colored lips;
■ Headache.

Plan of Action

If you suspect carbon monoxide poisoning:

■ Open all windows to obtain ventilation;
■ Turn off the engine and get fresh air;
■ Seek medical attention;
■ Have your car checked for exhaust leaks.

Chapter Thirty-One: Cardiopulmonary Resuscitation (CPR)

If an injured person stops breathing, or his heart stops, immediate treatment is needed. Without artificial respiration brain death may take place in a few minutes. Cardiopulmonary resuscitation (CPR) will provide artificial respiration while attempting to restart the heartbeat.

CPR Technique

1. Check mouth and throat for foreign material;
2. Clear airway;
3. Tilt head backward to prevent tongue from obstructing airway;
4. Place victim on a rigid surface;
5. Pinch nostrils and blow into victim's mouth with quick breaths;
6. Continuing blowing into mouth every 5 seconds (12 times per minute);
7. Feel wrist, groin or neck for a pulse;
8. If no pulse is felt, place the ball of your hand on the low part of the breastbone and compress every second.
9. Every five heart compressions should be accompained by one breathing procedure.

CPR is very tiring. Two people, one for breathing, one for heart compressions, make it easier. I recommend that every person over age 16 (and certainly every driver) should take a course in CPR, so that if an emergency arises you will be prepared for it.

Chapter Thirty-Two: Carsickness

Carsickness, or motion sickness, can occur in any age group. However, some people seem to be more susceptible to this syndrome, and precautions are advisable.

Symptoms

- Nausea;
- Vomiting;
- Light-headedness;
- Dizzyness;
- Lethargy.

This condition is caused by the motion of the vehicle, and the sight of scenery rapidly passing.

Treatment

1. Avoid looking at objects outside the vehicle;
2. Avoid looking at objects moving inside the car;
3. Focus on distant trees or the horizon;
4. Open window for fresh air;
5. Do not read while vehicle is moving;
6. Stop car and breath in fresh air;
7. Take carsickness medication.

Chapter Thirty-Three: Chest Injuries

Injuries to the chest wall are a common occurrence in head-on collisions. Often the driver, when not wearing a seatbelt, will be thrown violently into the steering wheel during a head-on crash.

There are two types of chest injuries, either open or closed. An open injury to the chest wall means that there is a break in the skin extending into the chest cavity. A closed wound may appear minor, but could include serious internal injuries.

Signs of Internal Injury

After a strong impact with the chest look for these signs of internal injury:

- Shortness of breath;
- Pain when breathing deeply;
- Coughing up blood;
- Bluish color to the fingernails or skin

Open Chest Wounds

Open injuries to the chest are often caused by rib fractures penetrating into the lung cavity, or through the skin. Open wounds to the chest can also be caused by a foreign object striking the body. These injuries can cause the lung cavity to fill with blood or cause the lungs to collapse.

Treatment of Open Chest Wounds

1. If a sucking sound is heard when breathing, place an impermeable material, such as vaseline gauze or plastic wrap, over the injury and secure with tape;

2. Seek medical assistance as soon as possible;

3. Use CPR (chapter 31), if necessary;

Closed Chest Injuries

Chest injuries that are closed can also cause breathing difficulties. Blood or fluid can accumulate in the chest cavity, severely impairing breathing.

A severe blow to the chest can cause broken ribs. The following are symptoms of broken ribs:

■ Localized pain and tenderness;
■ Pain when breathing deeply;
■ Victim prefers to lean to injured side.

Treatment for Broken Ribs

If you suspect that ribs are broken:

1. Find an ace bandage or tape.

2. Wrap the tape or bandage around the arm of the injured side, connecting the arm to the chest;

3. Seek medical attention.

Rib fractures generally do not constitute life-threatening emergencies. The fracture usually is well-stabilized by the muscles of the chest wall. Broken ribs which break the skin or penetrate the lung cavity are much more serious. Fortunately, most rib fractures are not of the serious type.

Chapter Thirty-Four: Diabetes

Diabetic emergencies are caused by either a high or a low blood sugar level. Frequently it is difficult to determine which extreme is present when a diabetic person becomes ill.

Signs and Symptoms

Common signs and symptoms of a diabetic emergency are:

- Sweet fruity, breath odor;
- Very dry or moist skin;
- Loss of consciousness;
- Altered state of mind;
- Breathing difficulties
- Rapid pulse.

If the person is conscious, ask if he took proper medication. Also ask what the person has eaten. A patient who has taken medication, but has not eaten, needs sugar. A patient has not taken medication, but has eaten a great deal, has an excessive sugar level.

Treatment

1. Give sugar to the person in the form of juice, soft-drink or candy. [It is much more dangerous to have a low-sugar level than to err on the side of too much sugar].

2. Give patient liquids because dehydration is a frequent problem;

3. Seek medical assistance.

Chapter Thirty-Five: Drowsiness—Warning Signs to Stop Driving

Drowsiness while driving a vehicle obviously can be a cause of catastrophe. Falling asleep at the wheel is responsible for thousands of motor vehicle accidents annually, many of which are fatal. Drowsiness is an avoidable problem if recognized and treated.

The following factors affect the degree of alertness:

- Duration of sleep;
- Alcohol consumption;
- Medication taken;
- Length of driving time;
- Time of day (night/daylight);
- Type of roadway;
- Whether traveling alone or with company.

At the first signs of falling asleep, take immediate action:

1. Change drivers, if possible;
2. Pull to the side of the road and take a nap;
3. Open the windows;
4. Turn up the radio;
5. Talk to the other passengers or sing to yourself;

To avoid situations where you might become drowsy:

1. Avoid drinking or medication before driving;

2. Avoid long drives on monotonous roads without planned stops;

3. Avoid driving during normal hours of sleep;

4. Plan to stop every 100 miles (160 kilometers) to stretch and have something non-alcoholic to drink;

5. Travel with a companion who is talkative.

Chapter Thirty-Six: Eye Injuries

Eye injuries must be attended to immediately to minimize permanent damage. Eye injuries can be blunt, from chemicals, or from sharp objects.

Blunt Injuries

Blunt injuries, when the eye is struck by a hard (but not sharp) object, can be much more serious than they appear externally. Hemorrhage can occur internally and its changes come on subtly.

Treatment of Blunt Injuries

1. Apply a cold compress to the injured eye;
2. Keep both eyes closed;
3. Obtain evaluation from an eye doctor (ophthalmologist).

Chemical Injuries

Acid from car batteries and other chemicals found in cars, can cause serious eye damage. Chemical injuries to the eye must be treated immediately.

Treatment of Chemical Injuries

1. Immediately flush the eye with cool water for ten minutes. Try to keep the other eye from being contaminated.
2. Do not rub the eyes;
3. Seek emergency medical attention.

Foreign Bodies in the Eye

Particles in the eye can be extremely uncomfortable. The particles can be eyelashes, insects, dust, or fragments of glass or metal. Any object that is embedded in the eyeball must be left alone until professional assistance can be obtained. Other particles can be removed carefully if they do not wash away by natural tearing.

Removing Particles from Eyes

1. **Avoid rubbing** the eyes;
2. Leave any penetrating fragment in place and cover both eyes;
3. Grab the eyelashes gently and pull the eyelids away from the eye.
4. Look for the particle;
5. Attempt to flush the particle with water;
6. If the object is on the lid, it can be removed gently with a cotton swab, handkerchief or tissue corner.

Cuts

Cuts to the eyeball or eyelids can be very serious. Treatment for cuts:

1. Cover the eye with sterile gauze compress;
2. **Do not press too firmly** as the inner contents of the eye may be expelled;
3. **Close both eyes** (motion of one eye causes motion of the other);
4. Obtain medical assistance at once.

Contact lenses: If an injury occurs to an eye with a contact lens in it, the lense should be removed by a trained professional.

Chapter Thirty-Seven: Head Injuries

All head injuries must be taken seriously. Significant brain or spinal cord damage can occur even when external injuries appear slight. In addition, when the head takes a direct blow, the neck is often affected.

Symptoms of serious head injuries:

- Altered consciousness:
    - [ ] coma
    - [ ] lethargy
    - [ ] confusion
    - [ ] restlessness
- Fluid draining from ears or nose;
- Bleeding from ears, nose or mouth;
- Headache;
- Nausea and vomiting;
- Unequal pupils of the eyes;
- Changes in speech

Treatment of Head Injuries

1. **Maintain** adequate **ventilation** by extending neck slightly backwards. Use CPR (Chapter 31) if necessary;

2. Keep the patient lying down and comfortable;

3. Withhold all food and drink;

4. Consider a possible neck injury. See Chapter 27. **Don't move the patient** unless absolutely necessary;

5. Seek medical attention immediately.

Chapter Thirty-Eight: Heart Attacks

Heart attacks are a life-threatening emergency and one of the leading causes of death in the world.

Symptoms of Heart Attacks

Typical symptoms of a heart attack are:

■ **Chest pain,** usually beneath the breast bone and not at the side of the chest. The pain is characterized as "squeezing" in nature;

■ Radiating **numbness**, heaviness, or **pain in the left arm;**

■ Shortness of breath;

■ Profuse **sweating** and anxiety;

■ **Nausea** or indigestion;

■ Generalized **weakness.**

Treatment

1. Determine whether victim can breath on his own;

2. Use CPR (Chapter 31) if victim is not breathing;

3. Loosen constrictive clothing, such as neckties, collar or scarf;

4. Keep the victim warm with blankets or towels;

5. Reassure victim that he will make it;

6. Obtain medical assistance.

Chapter Thirty-Nine:
Nausea and Vomiting

Nausea and vomiting have many possible causes. They may be caused by carsickness (Chapter 32), viral or bacterial infections, ulcers, excess alcohol intake, heart disease, stroke or emotional stress.

Some types of vomiting can be very serious. Signs of hemorrhage should signify the need for immediate medical help. Signs of internal bleeding are coughing up blood, or more commonly a "coffee-ground" appearing substance in the discharge.

Treatment

Treatment must be based on the suspected cause of the nausea. However, certain steps can be taken even when the specific cause is unknown:

1. Open a window for ventilation;
2. Stop automobile and get fresh air;
3. Avoid eating;
4. Take sips of carbonated beverage;
5. Seek medical attention if:
   - **Blood** present in discharge;
   - **Diarrhea** observed;
   - **Lips** are **cherry red;**
   - **Vomiting projected** with great force, several feet from patient.

Chapter Forty: Pregnancy

On occasion babies are born in cars, or taxicabs, on the way to the hospital. Labor can begin at any time, and occasionally is very short, particularly with second or later children.

If the pregnant woman cannot get to the health practitioner on time, several steps should be taken:

1. **Do not panic.** Before the advent of hospitals, women delivered very nicely on their own, or without doctors present;

2. Get the mother in a **comfortable position,** whether or her back, squatting or on her side;

3. Have a clean cloth ready to grab the baby as it emerges. The baby is very slippery;

4. After the baby has emerged, **do not tug on the cord;**

5. Clean the baby's face to assist breathing, and wrap baby in a blanket, towel or available clothing;

6. Give the baby to the mother to hold and await afterbirth (delivery of the placenta);

7. After delivery of the placenta, tie two strings or shoelaces on the umbilical cord, one about six inches from the baby, the other twelve inches from the child. Cut the cord between the two strings with a scissors or knife;

8. If the child is not breathing pat the baby gently on the back. If the child is still not breathing begin mouth-to-mouth resuscitation, covering the child's nose and mouth with your mouth;

9. Get mother and child to hospital. Keep baby warm.

Chapter Forty-One: Seizures

Epilepsy with seizures is a disease that is usually well-controlled. Occasionally a patient might have a seizure in an automobile.

Symptoms

■ Loss of consciousness;
■ Convulsions;
■ Spasms of the jaw—patient sometimes bites the tongue;
■ Loss of bowel or bladder control.

Seizures usually are self-limiting and last one to two minutes. It is most important to protect the patient from hurting himself.

Treatment

1. Do not attempt to restrict body motions;
2. Move objects that might harm the victim;
3. Place a soft, padded object between patient's teeth to keep tongue from being bitten. A piece of cloth or a handkerchief will suffice.
4. Loosen restrictive clothing, such as necktie and collar;
5. Turn patient's head to the side if vomiting occurs;
6. After seizure stops, seek medical assistance.

Chapter Forty-Two: Snowbound Survival

Whenever you drive out-of-town during the winter you run the risk of being snowbound. If you are driving during the cold months (including spring and fall in mountainous regions) bring emergency food, extra clothing and blankets with you. When snow starts falling heavily, start looking for shelter. Don't try to make it that extra twenty miles: pull off the road at a hotel or store.

Hypothermia

The human body cannot maintain its normal temperature when it is exposed to freezing temperatures for prolonged periods of time. **Hypothermia** is the result: a severe lowering of body temperature. Hypothermia is often fatal.

Snowbound Survival Procedures

If you find yourself stranded on a snowbound highway, take these steps:

1. **Cover your head.** Most heat loss occurs through the head;

2. Put on all clothing, blankets available;

3. **Signal for help.** Use your CB channels nine and 19. Put a red flag on the antenna. Start a fire, but not too close to the car. Light a flare;

4. Remove snow from exhaust pipe so that engine will run without allowing carbon monoxide to build up;

5. **Don't eat snow.** Eating or drinking ice cold fluids will reduce body temperature;

6. Heat ice, water, and food before ingesting. Your car's engine produces heat: use this heat to warm food and drink.

7. Use car heater intermittently. Base your use of engine on fuel supply;

8. **Eat candy** and food. This will help your body stay warm;

9. **Hug your fellow passengers.** Two people can keep each other warm;

10. **Don't venture out** unless you are well-dressed with insulated clothing and know the area. If you do venture out leave a map of where you were heading;

11. **Try to stay awake.** If you must sleep, sleep in shifts, so that one person is always looking for rescuers;

12. **Do not rub frozen body parts.** Put your cold hands or feet between thighs, or under an armpit to warm them.

Appendix
Emergency Driving

Brake Failure

1. Pump brakes to see if pressure returns.
2. Apply parking brake (unless you're on a curve—the result could be a spin).
3. Shift into lower gear.

Fire in Engine

1. Pull over and stop.
2. Turn off ignition.
3. Get out of car **IMMEDIATELY.**

Fog

DO NOT use your bright lights—the fog will reflect the beam back into your eyes.

Flooded Roads

If you **MUST** drive, do so slowly and in low gear.

Lightning/
Electrical Storm

Stay in your car—the body of your car will act as a deflector and pass the electrical current into the ground.

Skids

1. Do not apply brakes.
2. Remove foot from gas pedal.
3. Steer in the direction of the skid—this will straighten out the car.

Tire Blowout

1. Hang on tightly to steering wheel. The front end will vibrate when a front tire blows out, and the back end will vibrate when a back tire blows out.
2. **DO NOT** brake or you will lose control of the car.
3. Remove foot from gas pedal.
4. Carefully guide car to shoulder of road.
5. Do not try to drive further on a flat tire.